CERAMIC
TECHNIQUES

CERAMIC TECHNIQUES

Pravoslav Rada

HAMLYN

ACKNOWLEDGEMENTS

The publishers wish to thank the following people and organisations for their permission to reproduce photographs of the works belonging to them or of their property: Alšova jihočeská galérie, Hluboká nad Vltavou: Expozice keramiky, Bechyně (29); Edouard Chappalaz, Switzerland (31); Jean-Claude de Crousaz, Switzerland (32); Carmen Dionyse, Belgium (35); Otto Eckert, Czechoslovakia (XXIV); Fondation Maeght, Saint-Paul-de-Vence (XXI); Gerda Gruber, Mexico (24); Elly and Wilhelm Kuch, West Germany (XXIX); Eileen Lewenstein, England (56); Peteris Martinsons, Lithuanian SSR (30); Musée National Fernand Léger, Biot (XXXIII); Muzeum Narodowe, Warsaw (XXII); Náprstkovo muzeum, Prague (I, II, IV, V); Národní galerie, Prague (III, VIII—XIII, XV, 9, 16, 22, 33, 37, 38, 47, 60, 61); Národní muzeum, Prague: Národopisné muzeum (XVIII, 2, 3, 12, 13, 51—54, 57); Britt-Louise Sundell Nemes (8); Jan de Rooden, Netherlands (4); Johny Rolf, Netherlands (28); Karl Scheid, West Germany (XXVIII); Ursula Scheid, West Germany (XXXII); Vladimír Scheufler, Etnografický ústav ČSAV, Prague (45, 55); Immre Schrammel, Hungary (26); Klaus Schultze, West Germany (XXVII); Lubomír Šilar, Czechoslovakia (7); Lewis D. Snyder, USA (XXX); Kurt Spurey, Austria (27); Marta Taberyová, Czechoslovakia (XXXI); Lubor Těhník, Czechoslovakia (34); Uměleckoprůmyslové muzeum, Prague (VII, XVI, XVII, XIX, 1, 14, 15, 17—21, 25, 39, 40, 46, 48—50, 58, 62); Ida Vaculková, Czechoslovakia (11); Jindra Viková, Czechoslovakia (41); Ulla Viotti, Sweden (6); Carlo Zauli, Italy (XXIII); Bohuslav Zemánek, Czechoslovakia (43).
  Photographs of the works from Czechoslovak state and private collections and of working methods and techniques by Miroslav Hucek.

1 (*front endpaper*)
Plate
Casa Pirota, Faenza, Italy, 1540
Maiolica, pale blue glaze painted with *bianco sopra azzuro*; orange figure
Diameter 24.5 cm
Museum of Decorative Arts, Prague

2 (*back endpaper*)
Dish
South Bohemia, early 18th century
Pottery, blue glaze with white marbling
Diameter 28 cm
Ethnographical Museum, Prague

3 (*half-title page*)
Potter at wheel, saving box
Cheb region (Egerland), Bohemia, 19th century
Pottery, light brown body with transparent lead glaze, black painting
Height 28 cm
Ethnographical Museum, Prague

4 (*frontispiece*)
Cyclus VII
Jan de Rooden, Netherlands, 1982
Stoneware, blue and yellow body, unglazed; electrically fired at 1260 °C
Height 96 cm
Private collection

Designed and produced by Artia
First published 1989 by The Hamlyn Publishing Group Limited, a Division of The Octopus Publishing Group, Michelin House, 81 Fulham Road, London SW3 6RB
© Copyright Artia, Prague 1989
Ill. No. XXI © Copyright COSMOPRESS. Geneva 1989
Ills. Nos. XXII, XXXIII © Copyright SPADEM, Paris 1989
Text by Pravoslav Rada
Translated by Šimon Pellar
Drawings by Aleš Krejča
Graphic design by Aleš Krejča
ISBN 0-600-56154-2
Printed in Czechoslovakia by Polygrafia, Prague
2/12/04/51-01

CONTENTS

PREFACE

When selecting the subjects for the chapters of this book, I was guided by an awareness that it should be a technical guide for those creative artists who already devote themselves to ceramics or who intend to do so. The present publication is largely based on an earlier work of mine, which appeared in 1956 under the title Kniha o technikách keramiky (The Book of Ceramic Techniques), but this has been revised and supplemented with new material, especially a pictorial section. However, it would be beyond the scope of this book to include everything that comes under the heading of ceramics, since the subject is vast.

I have, therefore, attempted to cover those aspects of ceramics which are important for ceramic artists/craftsmen. With regard to working and decoration techniques used in the ceramic industry I have selected only those with which an industrial designer of ceramics should be familiar. Wherever ceramic manufacture utilizes techniques of other fields, such as graphics, printing or photography, the reader is referred to the literature relevant to those subjects. Only those methods and procedures which are specific to ceramics or which are used in a different manner are discussed in detail here. Of the many glaze and pigment formulae I have selected only those which either are not readily available on the market or which are of artistic or historical interest. Naturally, all these original recipes are intended as a guideline only and the potter is advised to test them or adjust them for materials available to him. Unless stipulated otherwise, all recipes are given in parts by weight.

I am fully aware of the fact that many professional potters will find some parts of this book redundant but since the publication is also intended for those who are inexperienced in the craft as well as for collectors and other people interested in ceramics, I felt the book should include basic facts.

I would like to thank all those who have helped in the making of this book, especially the staff of the following Prague museums: the National Museum, the Náprstek Museum, the Asian Collection of the National Gallery and the Museum of Decorative Arts, for their enthusiasm and invaluable help in compiling the pictorial material. My gratitude goes also to the staff of the Duchcov and Březová plants of the Carlsbad Porcelain Industries, as well as to the employees of the maiolica shops in Tupesy and Ratíškovice for their help in making the photographic records of working methods and procedures.

Pravoslav Rada

WHAT ARE CERAMICS?

5
Sitting Woman, burial pottery
Nayarid, Mexico, 1000-1300
Red clay, white slip, colloidal slip glaze
Height 38 cm
Private collection

The word 'ceramics' is derived from the Greek word *keramos,* which means potter's clay. Today, the term includes not only pottery but also all products made of clay and hardened by firing. The category thus encompasses such diverse products as bricks, porcelain dining sets, abrasive wheels, ceramic semiconductors and materials used in nuclear power plants or for the heat protection of space shuttles.

Ceramic wares can be classified according to various attributes. Usually they are divided into two large groups differing in the composition of the body. The first is represented by **heavy clay-ware**, that is, wares with a thick, coarse-grained, sometimes inhomogeneous, usually coloured body, for example, sewer pipes, furnace refractory linings, roof tiles, various brick wares, etc. Although even these materials are sometimes, albeit rarely, used in art ceramics, namely in architectural applications, this book will be concerned mainly with the second large group, namely **fine ceramics.**

In simple terms, fine ceramics are produced from ceramic materials with a particle size smaller than 0.05 mm. Fine ceramics are further classified according to the sintering of the body into **earthenware** (with an absorption capacity greater than five per cent), **semi-sintered wares** (up to five per cent) and **sintered wares** (absorption capacity up to two per cent).

RAW MATERIALS FOR CERAMIC BODIES

Plastic materials

The basic materials for the manufacture of utility and decorative ceramics are clays and kaolin; according to composition, use, firing temperature and deformation in fire they are distinguished as **brick**, **earthenware**, **porous (whiteware)**, **stoneware** and **porcelain** clays. They are used either directly or, more frequently, as components of man-made ceramic bodies. Components of ceramic working bodies are either **plastic** or **non-plastic.** The former include, for example, kaolin and primary and secondary clays, while non-plastic materials are, for example, quartz, feldspar, limestone, etc.

Plastic materials are fine-grained rocks formed by clay minerals whose particles are smaller than 2 mm in size. The basic property of these materials is their plasticity, that is, an ability to form a mouldable body when mixed with water. When bent, a piece of such material will not develop cracks and will retain its shape when dried and fired. A ceramic body composed only of plastic materials would, however, have a number of undesirable properties, for example, great shrinkage and poor drying of the body and it would also require high firing temperatures. **Grog** and **fluxes** are therefore added to the composition because these materials are non-plastic.

KAOLIN

The term kaolin was brought to Europe by the French Jesuit priest d'Entrecolles who went to China in the 18th century in search of the secret of porcelain manufacture. The word is derived from the Chinese *kao'ling*, which means a high ridge. Originally it was the name of the mountain where kaolin was mined.

Kaolin is a white, very soft, earthy material. It is dry to the touch and becomes fairly plastic when mixed with water. When fired, it retains its colour. Kaolin is fire-resistant (refractory). It is usually produced by weathering (kaolinization) of feldspathic rocks. Its basic component is the rock kaolinite $Al_2O_3 . 2SiO_2 . 2H_2O$. As a rule, kaolin is contaminated with remnants of unweathered parent rocks, especially quartz, feldspar or mica. While washing will remove the coarse-grained particles, fine grains of quartz sand, feldspar and mica will remain, and this should be taken into consideration when preparing a formula for a ceramic body. Quality porcelain kaolin must be as plastic as possible, have good dry strength and be white when fired. It must also cast well and have good binding power. To prepare a good, homogeneous working body, several kinds of kaolin and clay are usually mixed together and various liquefying agents are added to facilitate casting, for example, soda or water glass. Kaolin is used in the manufacture of porcelain and is added to other white ceramic bodies and engobes (slips).

PRIMARY CLAYS

Primary clays are a product of weathering of feldspathic rocks and are found at their original site of formation. They often contain substantial quantities of coarse particles of the parent rock and since the clay has not been waterborne there has been no opportunity for the selective sorting of particle sizes as in a secondary clay.

Primary clays are a mixture of clay minerals according to the exact composition of the parent rock and its means of decomposition. The most important to the potter are kaolinitic and montmorillonitic clay minerals. Bentonite, a highly plastic clay of very fine particle size, is a primary clay of volcanic origin whose main constituent is montmorillonite. Kaolin is the most important primary clay, valued for its purity and whiteness.

SECONDARY CLAYS

Secondary clays are clays which have been transported from their original site of formation. The main agent of transportation is water; however, wind and glacier-borne clays are known. The main pottery clays are those which have been deposited by water. The main effects of water transportation are:

1 grinding particles to a smaller size;
2 grading and sorting of fine from coarse particles;
3 mixing clays and minerals from various sites with the addition of organic materials.

It is not surprising therefore that secondary clays vary widely in their properties and composition.

Clays
Clays are usually classed by the ceramic products for which they are used, that is, as stoneware, earthenware, tileware, refractory, pottery and brick.

Fireclays
Fireclays withstand very high temperatures, usually at least 1580 °C. These refractory clays are used for linings of furnaces and for other technical purposes. Mixed with refractory schistose clays they are used for the manufacture of fireclay, which is known in some European countries as *chamotte.*

Stoneware clays
Stoneware clays are usually fired in the range 1200-1300 °C in such a way as to make their saturation coefficient (absorption) lower than five per cent by mass. It is important that the difference between the sintering point (saturation coefficient one per cent) and the melting point be at least five pyrometric cones, that is about 150 °C, otherwise the wares would easily lose shape and even melt altogether in the kiln.

Earthenware (whiteware) clays
Earthenware clays are usually fired in the range 1060-1200 °C. They fire to an ivory, yellowish or pure white colour; the body is porous, with an absorption of at least seven per cent. Highly plastic

6
Crackings in Our Time, relief
Ulla Viotti, Sweden, 1984
Stoneware clay with fireclay and rubbed pigment oxides; electrically fired at 1280 °C
60 × 80 cm. Private collection

kaolinitic clays with an admixture of montmorillonite are usually termed **ball clays**. Their plasticity is, among other things, caused by finely dispersed organic materials which give the clay a dark to black colour.

Brick clays
Brick clays are usually fired below 1100 °C. The body is porous and has a characteristic red colour caused by admixtures of iron compounds. The flux content is usually quite high and therefore their melting and sintering points differ only very little.

Marls
Marls contain more than twenty-five per cent finely dispersed limestone which functions as a highly effective flux. Since calcareous bodies have a very good body-to-glaze strength when combined with lead-tin glazes, marls are often added to tile, faience and other wares.

Bentonitic clays
Bentonitic clays are highly plastic materials of volcanic origin. Their most important constituent is montmorillonite ($Al_2O_3 . 4SiO_2 . nH_2O$). They are so plastic that an addition of a mere few per cent of this material greatly enhances the workability of ceramic bodies. They also improve the dry strength of shaped, unfired wares. A few per cent of bentonite added to the glaze will prevent settling of the latter at the bottom of the vessel.

7
Bird
Lubomír Šilar,
Czechoslovakia, 1984
Stoneware with fireclay,
light brown body with
rubbed pigment oxides
Height 60 cm, length
53 cm
Private collection

Non-plastic materials

FELDSPAR

Feldspar is a popular flux since, unlike limestone, it gradually improves the compactness of the body with increasing temperature. Like all powdered materials, ground feldspar makes the body 'leaner' and lowers its shrinkage during drying. On the other hand, it makes the body more compact at higher temperatures and, at the same time, increases the shrinkage. Since ceramic wares should have a uniform shrinkage, it is important always to add the same quantity of feldspar. The rule naturally applies to all ceramic materials.

Besides feldspar other materials are also used, for example, **pegmatites**, and recently ground feldspathic rocks like **granite**, **phonolite**, etc.

QUARTZ

Quartz is used either as ground lode quartz or as quartz (silica) sand. It must be fine-grained and as pure as possible in order to avoid an undesirable coloration of the body. Quartz makes ceramic bodies less plastic. Shrinkage caused by drying and firing is made much less pronounced by adding quartz grog. At the same time the melting point is lowered. For fine ceramic wares it is much better to use finely ground quartz rather than choosing sand.

LIMESTONE

Limestone is essentially a **calcium carbonate** (calcite $CaCO_3$) and is added to ceramic bodies in the form of ground limestone or floated whiting. During the drying stage, limestone acts as grog, while during the first phase of firing it also functions as grog, improving the porosity of the body, but acts as a fluxing agent during the later phases. If calcium carbonate is added in the form of ground limestone, the grinding must be very fine since heat converts limestone into quick lime. After firing, any large grains in the body are slaked, which increases their size, and this may cause chipping. The sintering and melting points of limestone lie quite close; even a slight overfiring may cause deformation, melting or bubbles.

GROG

Grog is fired clay, schistous clay, ceramic shards or fired kaolin ground to grains of various sizes depending on need and added in order to open the body. Grog increases the porosity and lowers the shrinkage during drying and firing. Ceramic working materials discussed in this book are grogged with fine-grained or powdered fireclay.

MAGNESIUM-BEARING MATERIALS

The most important magnesium-bearing ceramic materials include **talc** and **magnesite.** Both of these facilitate the formation of **cordierite** ($2MgO . 2Al_2O_3 . 5SiO_2$), which is characterized by a very low thermal expansion. This makes the product highly resistant to the effects of sudden temperature changes. Magnesium-bearing materials are, therefore, employed especially in electroceramics and wherever firing aids are used for quick firing. However, it must be borne in mind that the presence of MgO, as of quicklime (CaO) produced by limestone, shortens the sintering interval.

ORGANIC CONSTITUENTS

Sometimes various organic substances are added to ceramic bodies. One group, the so-called **lightening agents**, makes the fired body more porous and therefore lighter; other materials known as **plasticizers** artificially improve the plasticity of the ceramic batch and reduce moisture content.

Lightening agents (sometimes termed **expanders**) include peat, cork granule, sawdust, coal dust, starch or bran, usually finely ground. In order to disperse the material uniformly throughout the body, it is recommended to mix these ingredients with the dry batch and only then add the water, or to add the material dispersed finely in the mixing water. The organic substance burns out in fire, leaving the body porous, light and possibly with an attractive structure.

Plasticizers include dextrin (starch gum), gum arabic, glue, gelatine, paraffin oil, various waxes, methyl cellulose, polyvinyl alcohols, etc. They increase the plasticity of 'lean' or 'short' bodies or of batches in which plasticity cannot be achieved by adding plastic earths or in some other way. Plasticizers are used in porcelain bodies for hand modelling or throwing purposes. A very good plasticizer, albeit inorganic, is bentonite.

Ceramic batches and bodies

Most clays cannot be worked in a natural condition, that is, as they are found, but must first be processed by grinding, sieving, floating, grogging and mixing with other materials. Well-prepared ceramic batches should have the following properties:

1 Good working (shaping) property
The material should work well and should permit modelling and throwing and also bind fine grogging materials like sand, fireclay, etc.

2 Low shrinkage
High shrinkage usually results in warping, shattering or cracking of the wares during firing and sometimes even during the drying phase. Slips and glazes adhere poorly to such bodies and peel.

3 Glaze-body fit
The glaze must adhere well to the body, must not craze or peel, shiver or crawl or be absorbed by the body.

4 Retention of shape in fire
The wares must retain their shape when fired, and must not warp nor deform in any way.

5 Purity of raw materials
The individual constituents of the working batch must not contain impurities which could give the body an undesirable colouring, especially if the body is to be white, nor impair the body in any other way.

These basic properties of good ceramic working batches and bodies are supplemented by others, often as vital as the basic requirements listed above and including, for example, porosity, firing colour, casting quality, etc.

To achieve these requirements, particularly plasticity and low shrinkage, is sometimes quite difficult. Highly plastic materials fuse well but on the other hand show high shrinkage, which is undesirable. By adding fireclay grog or some other non-plastic material, even lean (short) secondary clays, the shrinkage can be lowered but this will also somewhat affect plasticity. The correct formula must, therefore, be tested beforehand.

8
Vase
Britt-Louise Sundell
Nemes, Sweden, 1978
Stoneware, white body,
black slip glaze, engraved
decoration; electrically
fired at 1175 °C
Diameter 18 cm
Private collection

Material testing

Ceramic materials are subjected to chemical, mechanical, physical and technological testing to assess their properties. For our purposes, just a few simple tests will suffice. They can be performed in the studio using only widely available aids. Detailed data on materials can be requested from the manufacturers.

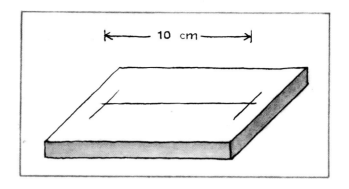

Fig. 1   Test clay tile, calibrated for measuring shrinkage

PLASTICITY TEST

The easiest way to test the plasticity of a clay is to mix it with water. A highly plastic, fat clay will mix poorly with water, while a non-plastic or lean (short) one will be thoroughly mixed within a short time or even immediately. An indicator of plasticity is the amount of water needed for mixing. Plastic clays require more water than non-plastic ones. Another way is to pour thinned clay on to a plaster-of-Paris slab and let it dry. A plastic clay will release water slowly, remain thin and adhere to the plaster longer than a lean clay. Another good test is to shape a small piece of clay into a roll as thick as a pencil. The longer you can make the roll, the more plastic and workable is the clay.

Plasticity is affected by various phenomena. When mixed with water, the material breaks into small particle clusters enveloped by a water film, with water remaining in the interstices between the individual clusters; this makes the clusters more movable in the mixed dough or paste. Plasticity is also enhanced by maturation or ageing, known as 'souring' by potters. Souring in fact means letting a moist clay rest to allow the moisture to penetrate even to the finest particles. Chinese potters used to bury clay in the ground for several years to let it sour.

Plasticity is also improved by the effect of organic decomposition and the action of micro-organisms; when your clay in the storage bin begins to smell, it may be a nuisance but it is also an indication of good souring. New batches can be 'soured' by adding old clay.

Plasticity of the body will be considerably improved by adding a highly plastic clay or bentonite. Just two or three per cent of bentonite will improve the workability of porcelain bodies by as much as fifty per cent.

SHRINKAGE TEST

Plastic clays and ceramic working batches will shrink during drying and firing. To assess the shrinkage, make a slab or bar from the batch to be tested. While the piece is still soft, mark it with a precisely measured distance, for example, 10 cm (fig. 1). Measure the distance after drying, fire the test piece and measure again. The shrinkage rate can be obtained using the following formula:

$$\frac{\text{original distance less distance after firing}}{\text{original distance}} \times 100.$$

The resulting figure represents the shrinkage rate in per cent. Note that the total shrinkage rate should not exceed eight to ten per cent.

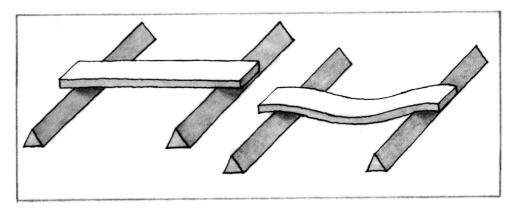

Fig. 2   Clay tile for testing meltability

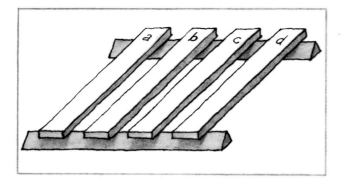

Fig. 3   Clay tiles for testing meltability

However, shrinkage does not depend only on the composition of the material and the batch but also on the method of working. For instance, cast wares show greater shrinkage than wares made of the same batch but moulded or thrown from a plastic clay or press moulded from an almost dry mix. It is, therefore, advisable to make the test piece by the same method as the intended ware. When testing a casting slip for shrinkage the reference distance must be inscribed on the mould.

FIRING TEMPERATURE

With every new clay it is imperative to test it for the temperature required to fire good bodies and then to adjust the composition to the firing temperature if necessary.

Prepare a test tile or strip about 15 cm long, 3.8 cm wide and 6 mm thick. Support the strip at both ends and place it in the kiln in such a way as to be able to observe it through the spyhole. The temperature at which the strip will start sagging in the centre is the maximum that the batch will withstand (fig. 2).

In most cases, the formula of the body must be adjusted to the firing temperature by adding some flux (low-melting clay, frit, ground glass, feldspar, etc.) or vice versa, that is, including more fire-resistant constituents in the formula.

When it is clear that the body will have to be adjusted, one must prepare a whole batch or series of test strips with a different percentage of flux or grog and fire them on the supports at the required temperature (fig. 3). The first unde-formed strip in the test series contains the right proportion of constituents. If your kiln permits it, fire at higher temperatures to establish the melting point of your batch. The difference between the sintering and melting points should be at least 150 °C.

Simultaneously with the firing test it is advisable to check body density. The simplest method of checking the quality of the body is by knocking on it and listening to the sound. The more compact or better fused the body, the clearer the ringing tone. However, a soaking test is much more precise. A precisely weighed fragment or potshard is boiled in water for three hours. When it is taken out of the water and dried, it is weighed again. The absorption can then be calculated as follows:

$$\frac{\text{weight of soaked piece less weight of dry piece}}{\text{weight of dry piece}} \times 100.$$

This gives the water absorption rate in per cent.

Sintered bodies have an absorption rate of up to one per cent, stoneware up to five per cent (technical stoneware up to seven and a half per cent) and porous wares over seven and a half per cent.

When adjusting the formula, the fired colour must also be taken into consideration. To make the colour of the body lighter, white materials like floated whiting or white porous clay are used. If the body is to be coloured, iron oxides, manganese compounds, coloured clays or other colorants are added to the formula.

LIME TEST

The presence of limestone particles in a clay is established by a test using sulphuric or hydrochloric acid. A few drops of the acid are deposited on to the crushed clay. If no foaming or effervescence is observed, the clay contains no limestone.

GLAZING TESTS

A test piece, preferably a pot, is glazed with a regularly used, reliable transparent glaze. Another piece is glazed with a quality opaque glaze. Crazing or shivering indicate that the shrinkage rates of the body and the glaze differ too much and must be better matched (for more detail concerning glazes and bodies see the chapter on glazes, page 43 ff.). One of the causes of faulty glazing may be too porous a body which may result in the latter soaking up the glaze. The porosity can be adjusted by grinding the materials to a finer particle size. On the other hand, if the porosity of the body is too low, it may be improved by using coarser-grained materials or by adding organic materials which incinerate during firing.

Preparation of clay for industrial use

The individual constituents of the working batch are first graded, cleaned, floated, ground, and hard rocks like feldspar or quartz are pre-fired and mechanically crushed. Dry materials prepared in this way are then weighed according to a well-proven formula and then ground for several hours in ball mills, which also ensures a thorough mixing. The drums of the mills are lined with silex or stoneware lining and filled to about one-third of their capacity with flint or ceramic balls. The impact of the rolling balls rubbing together and against the lining provides the milling action. The ground mixture is poured through a magnetic separator which removes fine iron particles and sometimes even some iron compounds. This is especially important in porcelain making because iron in the batch would produce brown stains and other flaws in the body.

Once the iron is separated, the mixture is fed into bins and transported to filter presses. Under pressure the excess water is separated from solid particles by thick cloth filters and drained, so that only a thickened mass known as **cake** remains. The cakes are then dried in drying ovens, ground and stored. Further processing includes kneading in de-airing pug mills (if the material is to be used for throwing) or mixing with a liquefying agent (deflocculant) to make casting slips.

9
Pair of Buffaloes
China, Chan dynasty, 1st century BC
Pottery with buff slicked slip
Height 16.5 and 25.5 cm
National Gallery, Prague

10
Sitting Figure
India (Bengal ?),
19th century
Buff body painted cold
with black, red, ochre and
white paint
Height 20 cm
Private collection

I
Goblet
Nasca, Peru, 200 BC-700 AD
Buff body, polished
coloured slip
Height 20 cm
Náprstek Museum, Prague

II
Dog, incense burner
Mexico, Colima culture, 1000—1300 AD
Red clay, slip glaze
Height 28 cm
Náprstek Museum, Prague

11
Bumblebee
Ida Vaculková, Czechoslovakia, 1982
Red body, white and red tin glaze; glost-fired
electrically at 1100 °C, then smoked in a ground-hog
kiln fired with wood. Height 29 cm. Private collection

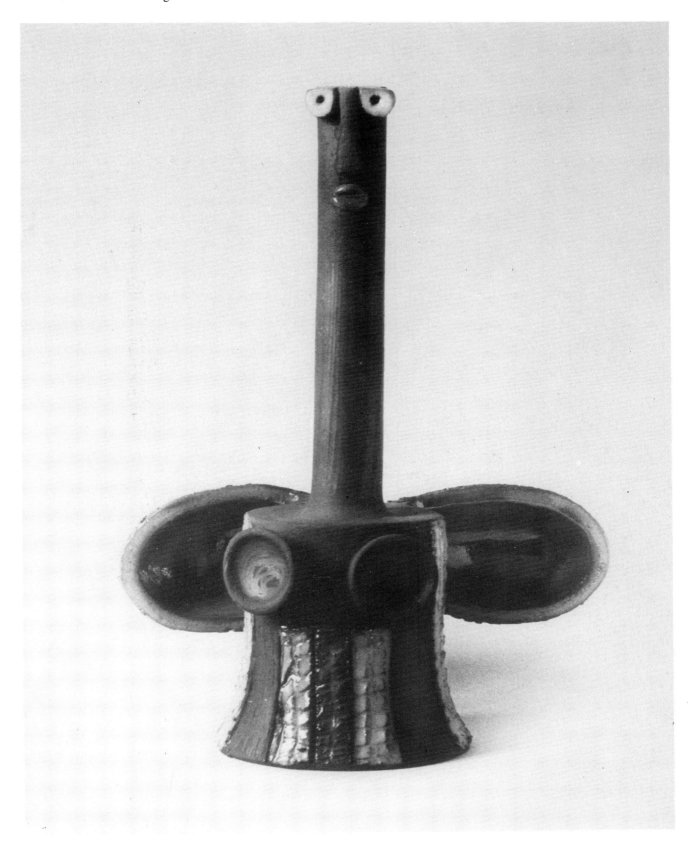

Preparation of clay
for studio use

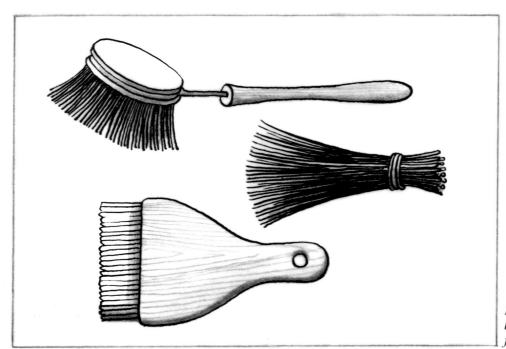

Fig. 4   Bristle and whisker brushes used for straining clay through a sieve

Fig. 5   Plaster or biscuit bats and a plaster mould for stiffening clay

In the studio, a working body or batch can be prepared quite simply and using a few tools. If a body is prepared only from primary or secondary clays, the necessary utensils include just a few buckets to soak the clay, something to mix it with and a flour sieve which is used to sieve the mixture several times. In order to force the clay through the sieve, small wicker brushes may be used but bristle brushes used for dishwashing will prove just as helpful (fig. 4). The sieved body is left to solidify in plaster moulds (fig. 5) and left in a bin to sour. Naturally, casting slips are not left to solidify. On the contrary, they are thinned with soda or some other deflocculant. Casting slips must be sieved several times to remove all lumps.

A traditional way of preparing the clay is to use large vats. The clay is mixed in a large wooden vat embedded in the ground. Next to the vat is a sloping trough covered with fine sand and boarded with fireclay slabs to absorb water. The mixed slip is sieved into a settling tank dug into the ground. The clay settles there and the water is partially absorbed by the ground, partially drained away.

A better system features two vats. One is filled with the mixture which is then sieved into the second vat and left to settle. The water lying on top is pumped back into the first vat and the settled clay still containing a relatively high percentage of water is then drained into a settling tank dug into the ground (fig. 6). Once the clay has solidified, it is

carved out in blocks and stored in storage bins.

When the clay is sufficiently soured, it is ready for further treatment. Prior to throwing, moulding or modelling the clay must be kneaded either manually or mechanically. Mechanical pugging is done with pug mills (fig. 7). These can be hand or roller fed and both can be vacuum de-aired.

However, some potters prefer to knead larger pieces of clay by hand or foot, or to beat it with

Fig. 6 Equipment for floating clay

wooden bats against a hardwood or stone slab. Smaller pieces are manually twisted, rolled, spread, pressed and kneaded as shown in figures 8 and 9.

This operation, known also as wedging, is extremely important, because the mechanical action blends the layers of different consistency, making the clay homogeneous and pliable, and what is most important, forcing air bubbles out of the

Fig. 7   De-aerator press (pug mill)

Fig. 8   Kneading clay by foot

Fig. 9   Kneading clay by wedging

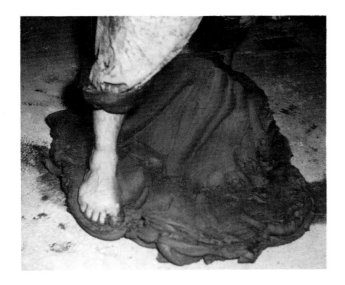

clay. A thorough preparation of the body will prevent flaws and waste during the later stages, that is, throwing and firing. Even a tiny air bubble can shatter or crack wares or shower adjacent pots in the kiln with slivers.

CLASSIFICATION OF CERAMICS ACCORDING TO BODY COMPOSITION

Soft ware (pottery)

Soft pottery includes all ceramic wares with a coloured, porous body, both glazed and unglazed. It includes not only typical pottery utensils but also special types of ceramic wares.

TERRACOTTA

The word is derived from the Italian *terra cotta,* meaning baked earth. The term generally signifies ceramic wares with an unglazed red-brown body, usually grogged with fireclay or even ground brick. Depending on the clay used, terracottas may be of brick, earthenware, stoneware and other types. Unglazed wares are termed **biscuit** or **bisque** (page 40).

Terracotta materials are used mainly for figural ceramics, reliefs and various other decorative and utility items.

However, the term is also used for antique wares made of this material. Typical examples are the so-called 'tanagras', or genre figurines, named after Tanagra in ancient Boeotia, where their manufacture culminated during the early Hellenic period. The figurines were mainly used in burial rites. They were fired in an oxidizing atmosphere at about 900 °C and, when cold, they were coloured with earthy pigments.

Terracottas also include other specific types of ceramics, for example, items made in South America in the pre-Columbian period.

Unglazed bodies are sometimes painted with colours in the bisque state. Folk art figurines decorated with this technique are very interesting artefacts. Recently ceramic artists, especially in the USA, have started using acrylic paints instead of ceramic colours on ceramic bodies.

SMOKED WARE

Smoked ware is a term used for unglazed pottery fired in primitive field kilns. When the required temperature (about 940 °C) is reached, wood containing a lot of pitch is thrown in the fire and the air inlet hole and all other vents are carefully sealed with clay. Today, naphtaline, tar, sawdust mixed with oil, or other smoky materials are also used. The smoke and the gases penetrate the ware, the soot remaining trapped in the body pores, which makes the ware less permeable.

Wares intended for smoking (also known as sawdust firing) are decorated by burnishing using hardwood, bone or stone tools. To improve the burnishing, bodies used for this type of technique should contain more plastic kaolinitic clays. The

12
Bear, tobacco box
Koloveč, Bohemia, late 19th century
Pottery, light brown body with transparent lead glaze, fur dark brown, coloured with brownstone
Height 18 cm
Ethnographical Museum, Prague

13
Milk pitcher
East Moravia, late 19th century
Smoked ware with burnished decoration
Height 24.5 cm
Ethnographical Museum, Prague

best way is to burnisch semi-dry bodies when they reach the so-called 'leather-hard' condition. Round wares are best burnished on a wheel. The fired smoked ware is matt grey in colour, with graphite-black shiny decoration.

The most difficult thing is to ensure that the smoke and gases permeate all pots in the kiln. This must be borne in mind when loading the kiln and the pots should not be stacked or lidded as customary in firing other types of wares. During the cooling one must also take care not to admit air to the kiln prematurely, because the deposited soot could ignite, or the wares dunt (crack).

One type of smoked ware is the Etruscan *bucchero nero* which used to be made from humus-rich secondary clays obtained from peat stripping. Peat was also used to fire the ware in a reducing atmosphere, that is, without access of air. The burnt humus was retained in the body as black carbon.

The technique can be imitated even in a regular kiln. The ware is made from clay mixed with 10-15 per cent ground charcoal, placed in a saggar (case of baked fireproof clay), covered with charcoal or coke grit, sealed and then fired at 900 °C.

TERRA SIGILLATA

Until recently the composition and manufacturing technique of black painted Grecian vases and reddish brown Roman pots decorated with figural reliefs and known as *terra sigillata* remained a mystery.

The matt surface shine, typical of these wares fired at about 1000 °C, was imitated by burnishing or varnishing the body. Today, however, we know that the lustre was produced by a thin layer of glaze prepared from a colloidal solution of illitic iron-bearing clay. The relief decorations were stamped into the soft body by stamp dies made from fired clay. In later periods these wares received their name from their striking similarity with sealing wax, both in colour and decoration.

A glaze for *terra sigillata* can be prepared according to a recipe developed by J. B. Kenny: 1000 g illitic clay (of the same composition as that used for the body) and 1000 g rainwater is ground

14
Goblet
Italy, Etruscan period, mid-6th century BC
Bucchero nero ware
Height 11 cm
Museum of Decorative Arts, Prague

15
Oil jars (*Lekhytos*)
Greece, 4th century BC
Red body, white slip, black colloidal glaze
Height 12 and 14 cm
Museum of Decorative Arts, Prague

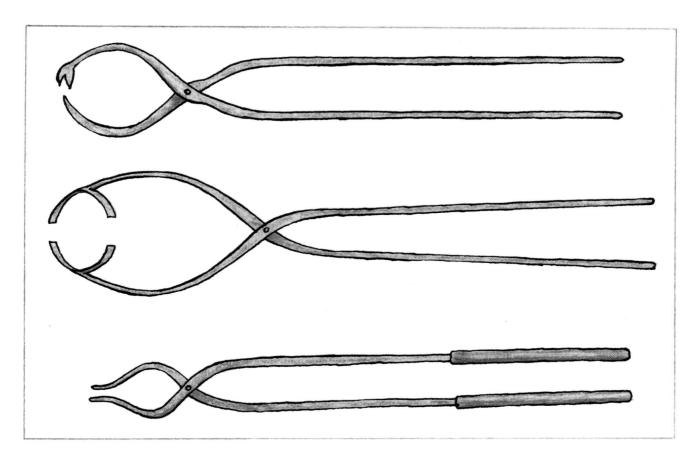

Fig. 10   Raku tongs

in a jar mill for 24 hours or longer. The mixture is then poured into a narrow, tall glass vessel and topped with rainwater to make its specific weight 1.2 g. Then 20 g sodium hydroxide is added and the mixture is left standing for more than 24 hours. An almost transparent liquid will remain above the sedimented clay, but the liquid still contains clay in colloidal state. The liquid is carefully drained into another vessel and applied to the touchdry or dried but unfired body. The surface of the fired ware is very hard and has a slight velvety sheen. Firing is of utmost importance. The atmosphere must be fully oxidizing and the temperature about 900 °C. The first results are often disappointing since not all clays can be used for *terra sigillata*.

The black and red painted **Grecian vases** and the Roman *terra nigra* wares used to be made similarly to the *terra sigillata* wares. The ornaments and figural motifs were painted with an illitic colloidal substance on a calcareous body fired yellow or red. What is different, however, is the method of firing. The ware is first fired in

16
Bowl with Fuji motif
Kyoto, Japan, 18th century
Raku ware with white and black glaze
Height 8 cm, diameter 12 cm
National Gallery, Prague

25

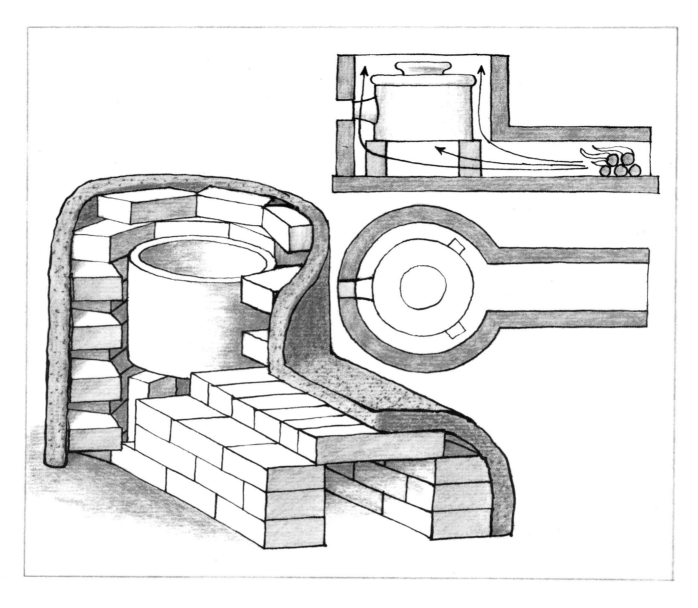

Fig. 11 Schematic diagram of a raku kiln

a strongly reducing atmosphere to about 850 °C and then cooled in a reducing atmosphere to about 700 °C. Further cooling must take place in an oxidizing atmosphere to make the places not covered by the colloidal substance re-oxidize to the original colour.

A similar method was used for firing black **graphite clay pottery** of the La Tene period, or the pottery of the Hallstatt culture, featuring a black graphite decoration. These techniques can be imitated by using a body containing 85 per cent iron-bearing clay and 15 per cent graphite and a slip made from 90 per cent illitic clay and 10 per cent graphite.

JAPANESE RAKU WARE

Raku is a term applied in Japan for wares used mainly for serving and drinking tea. The first raku was made in Kyoto in the 16th century by the potter Chojiro (1516-92) who had been inspired by the local tea master Rikyu (1521-91). The name *raku* was given to this type of pottery by the military ruler Toyotomi Hideyoshi, and the younger brother of the inventor, Jokei, accepted it as his family name. Raku pottery has been made in Kyoto by fourteen successive generations of potters and since the time of Raku III, Donyu († 1656), it has been made in the same house which has survived until today. In Japanese, *raku* means 'felicity'.

Raku was introduced to the West by Bernard Leach, who spent many years in Japan. Leach described the manufacture of red raku, known as *aka*, and black raku, called *kuro*. Since the body of both raku types must withstand abrupt changes of temperature, 25-30 per cent fireclay is added to the batch.

Red raku is made by applying a thick layer of ochre to a biscuit-fired body. The biscuit is then given a coat of transparent raku glaze and glost-fired to about 850 °C. The colour differs according to the grade of ochre and the thickness of the glaze layer. A deep salmon pink is considered to be the most exquisite of raku reds.

Black raku pottery is glazed with a thick layer of lead-iron glaze fired in a reducing atmosphere at about 1100-1200 °C. Both raku wares are fired in a special raku kiln (fig. 11), although a regular kiln may be adapted to permit the ware to be taken out when the temperature reaches the required point, since the fired ware must be quenched immediately in cold water.

Prior to cooling in water the temperature of the heated ware may be lowered in places by throwing the pot into wood shavings, sawdust or sawdust mixed with oil, or by wrapping it in oiled rags. This will produce peculiar colour shades and lustre effects. According to Leach, the scars left in the glaze by tongs are regarded as a positive feature. Another desirable characteristic feature of raku pottery is crazing.

When the first item has been removed from the kiln using tongs (fig. 10), another may be placed inside immediately. Naturally, the temperature drops when the door is opened, but after the correct point has been reached again, the item is fired for about 20 minutes and then removed. In this way, firing may go on continuously. Raku glazes are discussed in the chapter on glazes.

MAIOLICA AND FAIENCE

The two terms are used for the same type of ware, characterized by a porous body covered with an opaque lead-tin glaze.

In the 15th century the Balearic Islands in the Mediterranean became a major centre of ceramic manufacture, first established there by the Arabs. The dining wares exported from the islands to Italy in the 15th century came to by called **maiolica**, a derivation of Majorca, the name of the largest island of the group. The term **faience** comes from Faenza, a town near Bologna and a major manufacturing centre of ceramic wares in 16th-century Italy.

Literature, however, does not clearly distinguish the two. According to the origin of the ware,

17
Artichoke and Asparagus butter dishes
Holíč, Slovakia, 1760-70
Faience with painting on fired glaze; Artichoke turquoise green, Asparagus pale yellow, with green tips, drawing in manganese
Height: Artichoke 15 cm, Asparagus 21 cm
Museum of Decorative Arts, Prague

18
Pot
Moravia, Czechoslovakia,
1616
Habaner faience with
pewter lip and spout,
white tin glaze, drawing in
cobalt and manganese
Height 26.5 cm
Museum of Decorative
Arts, Prague

the term maiolica should be used for wares with a coloured body and an opaque coloured glaze; faience should be reserved for wares with a light-coloured calcareous body and a white opaque glaze, for which Faenza was famous. The situation became confused during the 19th and early 20th centuries because the English and Germans started manufacturing slipware and other ceramic wares under the name maiolica.

The usual custom today is to use the term faience for all wares of this type regardless of origin, while maiolica is reserved for Italian faience wares. The body of these wares is made from strongly calcareous clays or normal secondary clays with 10-40 per cent whiting. The typical decoration is painting into a raw enamel (glaze). The firing temperature is 950-980 °C. Literature terms such wares faience with 'high' fire glazes, as compared with faience decorated with painting on to a fired glaze (using the so-called muffle colours) and refired at 700-800 °C, a technique developed originally in Delft, Holland, at the end of the 17th century.

To list all the places and people famous for faience manufacture is beyond the scope of this book, since such a list would have to include practically all the countries in the Far East, Hispano-Moorish maiolica, Faenza in Italy, the family of della Robbia, Francesco Xanto Avelli, Bernard Palissy of France, the famous Delft wares from Holland or faience made by the Anabaptist refugees who settled in Moravia and Slovakia and became known as the Habaner.

Earthenware (whiteware)

Earthenware was allegedly invented by John Astbury of Staffordshire who, in the early 18th century, manufactured the first **creamware** later made famous by Josiah Wedgwood. The earthenware body is porous and composed of white-firing whiteware clays with an iron content lower than one per cent, and kaolin, feldspar, quartz and limestone. According to the composition and compactness of the body earthenware is divided into soft (calcareous), hard (feldspathic) and medium-hard (mixed). Hard earthenware sometimes approaches stoneware in composition, compactness of the body and firing temperature.

Unlike other ceramic wares, biscuit earthenware is fired at the same, or even higher, temperature than that of the glost-fire to prevent crazing of the glaze to which calcareous bodies are prone. Today, earthenware is used mainly for sanitary tiles and tableware.

WEDGWOOD WARE

Josiah Wedgwood (1730-95) started as a creamware manufacturer but gradually added other wares to his range, for example, red stoneware (*rosso antico*), **black basalt (Egyptian black)** and also coloured stonewares named after their appearance — **jasper, porphyry, agate, marble** and **cane wares**.

The characteristic decoration of Wedgwood ware is Classicist reliefs luted to a coloured surface. These cameos are known in the trade as sprigs and were originally white but later also coloured. These flat reliefs are made in plaster moulds and then luted to the dried body with slip and gum arabic.

Most Wedgwood recipes are taken from existing records. Some were even printed in a booklet which Wedgwood published under the title *Experimental Book.*

19
Cup with sugar bowl
Staffordshire, England,
18th century
Wedgwood ware (black basalt), black coloured body
Height: bowl 14 cm,
cup 6.5 cm
Museum of Decorative
Arts, Prague

20
Goblet with lid
Staffordshire, England,
18th century
Wedgwood ware (jasper
ware), blue body with
white cameo decoration
Height 25 cm
Museum of Decorative
Arts, Prague

Queen's ware		Black basalt ware		Cane ware		Jasper ware	
Flint	2	Etruria iron marl	6	Purbeck clay	20	Burnt flint	4
Feldspar	3	Chesterton fired		Common clay	4	Cawk*	24
Plaster-of-Paris	2	iron ore	2	Burnt flint	5	St Steven's clay	7
Kaolin	1	Black oxide of		Alabaster	3	Purbeck clay	13
		manganese	1	Limestone	$1/2$	Alabaster	1
				Enamel	$1/16$		

(Note: As elsewhere is this book the figures signify parts by weight.)

* Cawk is a Derbyshire chalk substance containing barium sulphate.

Wedgwood also manufactured solid jasper and jasper-dip wares with a white body covered with a coloured slip.

Blue body		Black body	
Purbeck clay	6	Purbeck clay	12
Enamel*	1	Alabaster	6
Alabaster	2	Ochre	6
White lead	1	Manganese	2

* Cobalt-potassium silicate (blueing)

Agate ware glaze		Body for white figurines	
White lead	120	Burnt flint	1
Burnt flint	30	Cawk	24
Copper oxide	9	Cornish clay	7
		Purbeck clay	13
		Alabaster	1

Mazarine blue			
Enamel	16	Frit, to which add:	
Borax	2		
Red lead	8	Red lead	2
Potassium nitrate	2	Enamel	3
		Cobalt glass	1

Wedgwood wares were imitated widely not only in England but also by manufacturers in various countries all over Europe.

SOFT STONEWARE (OVENWARE)

This is not genuine stoneware, since the body is still partially porous, although the firing temperature often exceeds 1250 °C. Unlike soft pottery it is considerably fire-resistant and can be used for cooking on a naked flame. It is typically decorated with slip glazes.

Some interesting examples of this type of ceramic ware are the so-called Bolesław tankards, made in the town of Bolesław in Polish Silesia. They used to be very popular because they were quite resistant to temperature changes. This was because the body was made from fireclay, sand and 25 per cent magnesite. The slip glaze, made from local clays, was fired in a reducing atmosphere to 1260-1300 °C. Slow cooling gave the glaze a characteristic brownish colour.

21
Pitcher
Bolesław, Poland, 18th century
Stoneware with typical coffee-coloured (Bolesław brown) slip glaze and white reliefs
Height 17.5 cm
Museum of Decorative Arts, Prague

Stoneware

Together with porcelain, stoneware ranks among wares characterized by a dense (compact) body, that is, with an absorption rate lower than five per cent. The body may be either coloured or white but white stoneware is also termed porcelain stoneware. The basic materials for stoneware manufacture are stoneware clays mixed with other constituents like feldspar, quartz, fireclay, etc. Apart from typical salt glazes, aluminous, feldspathic and lead-feldspar glazes are used. The firing temperature ranges between 1200 and 1280 °C, depending on the composition of the body.

Stoneware probably originated in China, where it was made as early as the 7th century BC. Chinese stoneware with coloured reduction glazes, known in Europe as **celadon**, *sang de boeuf*, etc., has never been surpassed in perfection. In Europe stoneware first appeared in the 11th century in Germany where its manufacture flourished most during the 15th and 16th centuries. From Germany the art of stoneware manufacture spread throughout the continent.

There is no sharp dividing line between hard porous ware, white stoneware and porcelain. Good examples of this are some types of Wedgwood ware which border on stoneware. An example of a transitional product between stoneware and porcelain is **vitreous china**, which has a vitrified, white-firing, yet not translucent body.

VITREOUS CHINA

Vitreous china is one of the most recent inventions in the trade. It was first made in the 1920s in the USA, where it is frequently used for standard tableware.

BÖTTGER STONEWARE

In 1707, when searching for a formula for genuine porcelain, Johann Friedrich Böttger chanced upon red stoneware of the Chinese Yi-hsing type. These products ranked among the most luxurious and fashionable wares of the day and were further perfected by grinding, burnishing and engraving on glass cutting machines, setting in precious metals and being decorated with mother-of-pearl, ivory, pearls or enamel.

Although the original formula had not survived, the Meissen Porcelain Works re-established the manufacture of these wares after 1922. The formula was derived from chemical analyses of original Böttger wares.

22
Octagonal box
Ri, Korea, 18th century
Glazed stoneware, white and brown slip
Height 13 cm, diameter 20 cm
National Gallery, Prague

23
Teapot
Kuan-Tung (Canton), China, 18th century
Unglazed stoneware, dark red body
Length 22 cm
Private collection

Formula after Berdel

A

		Body fired at
Plastic porous ware clay	35	1280-1350 °C, glazed
Kaolin	20	with lead-boron glaze
Feldspar	17	and glost-fired at
Silica sand	28	1180 °C.

B

		Biscuit fired at about
Plastic porous ware clay	58	940 °C, glazed with
Feldspar	20	glaze for soft porcelain
Silica sand	22	and glost-fired at
		1280-1350 °C.

Formula after Schätzer

		Body fired at
White porous ware clay	24	1250-80 °C, glazed
Kaolin	25	with lead-boron glaze
Feldspar	24	and glost-fired at
Ground quartz	22	1180 °C.
Finely ground potshard	5	

Formula for ironstone china

(used mainly for unglazed teaware, origin of the formula unknown; in a different proportion)

Kaolin	120	150	500	600	100	250
Blue stoneware clay	60	100	300	—	180	150
Cornish stone (pegmatite)	180	200	700	600	600	400
Flint	80	120	250	400	60	75

Porcelain

The body of porcelain is vitrified to a higher degree than stoneware and, if thin, it is translucent. Hard and soft porcelains are distinguished by the firing temperature.

Hard (European) porcelains are fired at 1350-1500 °C. Soft porcelains include Asian wares with a firing temperature of about 1300 °C, English bone china fired at 1220-1300 °C, and frit porcelain which has a firing temperature of about 1100 °C.

CLASSIFICATION OF PORCELAIN ACCORDING TO BODY COMPOSITION
(after Kallauner)

PORCELAIN	HARD				SOFT			
Constituents, in %	Normal	For medium fire	Seger	New Sèvres 1881	Bone	Frit	Chinese	Unglazed parian
Kaolin or clay	40-60	40-43	30	40	25-40	25-50	32	40
Feldspar	20-30	25-30	27	35	25-60	max. 45	37	66
Quartz	20-40	30-35	43	25	—	max. 35	31	—
Bone ash	—	—	—	—	10-40	—	—	—
Frit	—	—	—	—	—	5-55	—	—

Porcelain first appeared in China (its common name 'china' in English derives from Persian *chīnī*) in the 7th century during the rule of the T'ang dynasty. It reached Europe via Palestine during the Crusades and was literally worth its weight in gold. It was admired not only for its elegance but many people also ascribed to it magical power. It was a common belief that poisoned drink would shatter the cup. When Marco Polo brought the first more detailed reports of porcelain manufacture in 1295, attempts were immediately made to imitate it but a major breakthrough came only as late as the end of the 17th century when manufacture of soft frit porcelain started in Saint-Cloud, France. The formula for hard porcelain was discovered only in 1709 by Johann Friedrich Böttger in Meissen, Saxony. Although the formula was a closely-guarded secret, porcelain manufacture soon spread to many European countries.

FRIT PORCELAIN

In the mid-18th century frit porcelain manufactured under the name *pâte tendre artificielle* at Sèvres, France, became famous throughout the world. The formula, however, had been invented earlier in 1673 by Louis Poterat of Rouen and Pierre Chicaneau manufactured it as early as 1695 in his Saint-Cloud factory.

The body composition was as follows (according to Pukall):

Potassium nitrate	22.0		
Sodium chloride	7.2		
Potassium aluminium sulphate	3.6	Frit	75
Sodium carbonate	3.6	Floated	
Calcium sulphate	3.6	whiting	17
Silicon dioxide (silica)	60.0	Marl	8

The frit is washed in hot water and then finely ground. Enough soft (green) soap or gum arabic is added to give it sufficient plasticity. Still, such mixture takes poorly to hand building and the batch is better moulded or cast in plaster moulds where it is left until dry. The body is then biscuit-fired until completely vitrified, that is, to 1200-1300 °C, depending on the formula. In order to prevent deformation, the biscuit is fired covered with powdered quartz. The biscuit fired

III
Chen-Mu Shou Tomb Guardian
China, T'ang dynasty, early 8th century
Pottery with three colour glaze
Height 75.5 cm
National Gallery, Prague

IV
Ceramic cover
Sepiko, New Guinea, 19th century
Buff body, red and white slip
Height 21 cm
Náprstek Museum, Prague

V
Ancestor, burial pottery
Agui, Ghana, 20th century
Red clay, black and white slip
Height 31 cm
Náprstek Museum, Prague

in this way is then coated with a glaze which melts at a lower temperature of about 1100 °C. The glaze must contain glue, or it would not adhere to the body, which is completely vitreous.

BONE CHINA

Bone china received its name from the main constituent of the batch, bone ash. It was invented in 1748 by Thomas Frye, an Englishman, and improved and marketed commercially by Josiah Spode of Stoke-on-Trent in 1790. One of its major advantages is its high translucence but bone china generally fails to equal hard porcelain in technical parameters.

24
Aleteo
Gerda Gruber, Mexico, 1980
Bone china, clay with fireclay, wood; electrically fired at 1280 °C
Height 45 cm
Museum of Modern Art, Mexico City

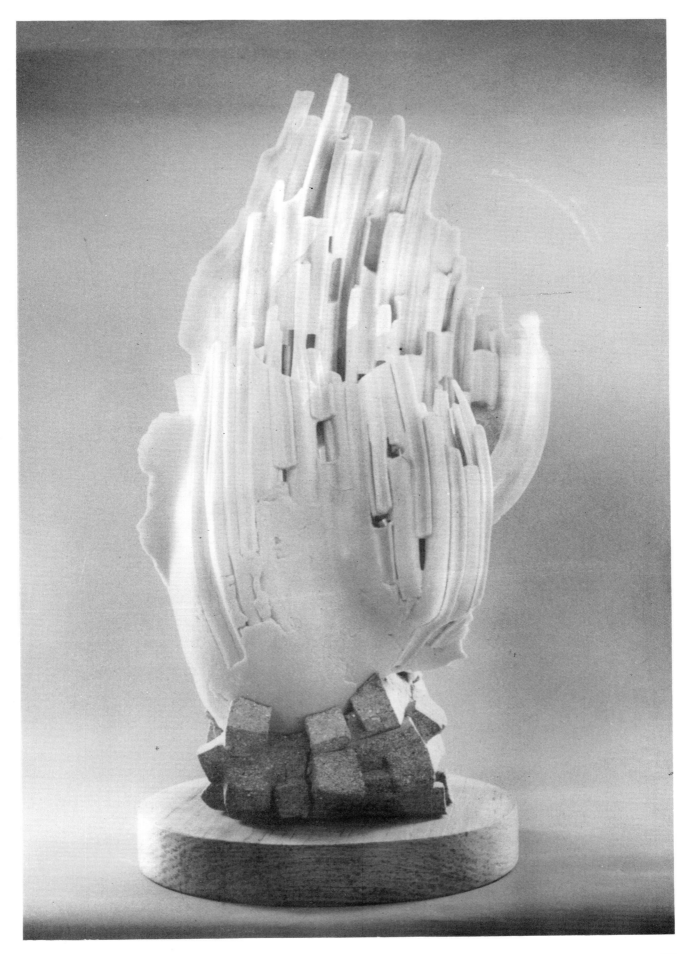

Bone china formula after Budnikov

Kaolinite	45	Kaolinite is introduced
Feldspar	5	in the form of
Bone ash	40	whiteware clays or
Quartz	10	china clays, quartz and
		feldspar in the form of
		pegmatite.

As with frit porcelain, the biscuit is fired covered with powdered quartz at 1280-1300 °C, that is until the body is completely vitrified.

The body is then glazed with a glaze based on the following formula:

Feldspar	38 ⎫	Frit	60
Boric acid	27 ⎪	Feldspar	20
Quartz	24 ⎬	White lead	20
Floated whiting	11 ⎭		

The glost-firing temperature is 1100-1150 °C. Apart from the usual methods of glazing, the glaze can be also applied by sprinkling the powdered glaze on to the body coated with an adhesive sticky oil film.

Thin-bodied pots are manufactured in the following way: the body is first thrown normally, dried and then turned on a lathe to produce a thin wall. The method is used not only for bone china but also for Wedgwood wares (see page 29).

BISCUIT PORCELAIN (PARIAN)

Bone china factories produced ceramic figurines from a special material fired without a glaze. This type of porcelain is sometimes also termed **carrara** or **parian**, because it resembles in appearance marbles quarried in Carrara, Italy, and on the island of Paros. Biscuit was first made in 1844 in Stoke-on-Trent, England, and was used mainly for copies of classic figural work.

The term **biscuit** (or **bisque**, which is sometimes also used) means 'twice-fired' and generated from the technological procedure used in the manufacture of statuettes. These were first cast in moulds, retouched and fired, retouched again and refired (again without a glaze) at a high temperature. To prevent deformation, the figures must be properly supported by kiln furniture made from the same material.

According to W. Pukall, parian contains 60 per cent feldspar and 40 per cent kaolin. Seger gives the formula for Copenhagen biscuit as follows: 45 per cent feldspar, 54 per cent kaolin and one per cent ground marble. It is fired at 1280-1300 °C.

25
Psyche
Royal Porcelain Factory, Copenhagen, Denmark, after 1867
Biscuit porcelain (after a sculpture by B. Thorvaldsen, 1811)
Height 31 cm
Museum of Decorative Arts, Prague

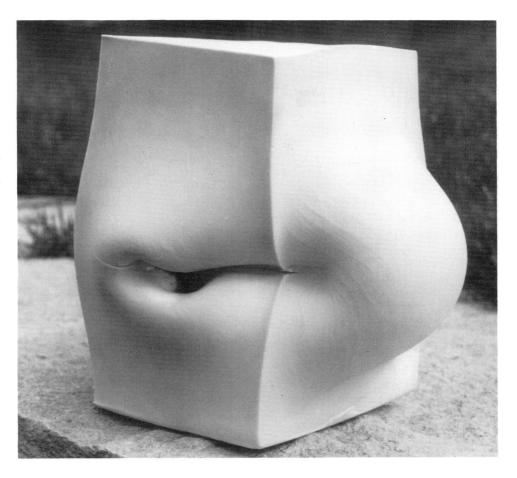

26
Porcelain cube
Imre Schrammel, Hungary,
1982
Biscuit porcelain deformed
by a shot from a small
calibre pistol while still
plastic; gas-fired at
1380 °C
Height 15 cm
Private collection

The kaolin used must contain as little quartz as possible, since quartz produces undesirable shiny spots on the fired surface. Because some manufacturers also made biscuit from regular porcelain bodies, they had to etch away the surface lustre with acid.

English manufacturers also used to make coloured biscuit wares. The body was coloured with pigment oxides and decorated with white slip (using the so-called *pâte-sur-pâte* technique, see page 147) or with porcelain enamels applied on to the unglazed body (*émaux sur bisque*).

For large figural work, parian bodies with an addition of frit were used. Below is a formula given by Budnikov:

Silica sand	52	Frit	—	24
Feldspar	23	Kaolin	33	36
Pegmatite	10	Feldspar	45	—
Potash	15	Pegmatite	22	—

The firing temperature range is 1250-1300 °C.

OTHER SOFT PORCELAIN

Although Böttger had succeeded in unveiling the mystery of porcelain manufacture, efforts were still made to find new formulae. Experimenters sought porcelains with a lower firing temperature, that is, East Asian porcelain wares, which would offer greater possibilities for using colour as a menas of decoration.

Seger porcelain
Seger porcelain is a highly translucent porcelain of yellowish colour. It was discovered in 1880 by Hermann August Seger (1839-93), whose other inventions included the Seger pyrometric cones. Seger kept the formula for his porcelain secret at first but later decided to make it public. It was composed of 31 per cent Lötheiner clay, 39 per cent sand and 30 per cent feldspar. The biscuit was fired at 950 °C, the glaze at 1280-1300 °C.

At about the same time the factory in Sèvres, France, introduced the so-called **new Sèvres china** (*pâte nouvelle*), composed of 40 parts kaolin, 35 parts feldspar and 25 parts quartz, and fired at a temperature of 1280 °C.

Soft East Asian porcelains
These are made from china clays rich in flux. Unlike hard European wares, Asian porcelains contain less clay and more feldspar and quartz. In China and Japan porcelain wares are thrown on the wheel, which is facilitated by the considerable plasticity of the dough, caused primarily by mica. Another difference is that the glaze is applied on to an unfired body, then hard-fired to 1280 °C.

HARD PORCELAIN

A typical hard porcelain paste contains 50 per cent kaolin, 25 per cent quartz and 25 per cent feldspar. This general formula is used as a base for new pastes and the ratio of the individual components is adjusted according to fired specimens until the body is perfect in all respects.

Porcelain glaze is composed of the same materials but contains more flux. When fired, it produces a hard surface layer fused with the body by means of a transition zone. In this respect it differs from glazes of some soft porcelains which adhere to the body as a sort of coating.

Porcelain pastes can be coloured with oxides or salts of various metals. The colour range of soft porcelain is much greater than that of hard porcelain. In the case of the latter the range is limited by the firing temperature and the reducing atmosphere in the kiln.

Listed below are some coloured paste formulae (after Hegemann).

Light to dark blue	95-85%	basic paste	+5-15%	cobalt monoxide
Bluish green	85%	basic paste	+ 5%	cobalt monoxide
Dark green	85%	basic paste	+10%	chromic oxide
Green	98%	basic paste	+ 2%	chromic oxide
Ivory	98%	basic paste	+ 2%	manganese dioxide

GLAZES

Glaze materials

As can be judged from their name and appearance, glazes chemically resemble glasses. They are glassy coats covering the surface of ceramic bodies, rendering them impervious to water and easy to clean, improving their mechanical strength and at the same time playing an important role as a decorative factor.

Glazes can be classified according to **colour** (coloured and colourless), **translucence** (transparent and opaque), **lustre** (glossy, semi-matt or matt), **meltability** (low-melting, that is soft, up to 1200 °C, and high-melting, that is hard, above 1200 °C), **method of processing** (fritted and unfritted, that is raw), **chemical composition** (boric, lead, feldspathic, salt, aluminous, etc.), but they can also be distinguished according to **appearance**, **decorative properties**, etc.

Glazes are essentially glasses, composed of quartz and oxides of various metals which melt with heat. When combined with silica, they are termed silicates; a lead glaze is in fact a lead silicate. Silicon dioxide as an acid component of the glaze can be partially replaced by boric acid; such glazes are borosilicates in chemical terms.

The most important materials used for glaze formulation include the following:

QUARTZ

Quartz is the chief constituent of glazes since it is the main source of silicon dioxide SiO_2. It is vital to have it as pure as possible, without colouring pigments such as iron, which turn glazes brown. The most frequently used sources of silicon dioxide are pure lode quartz or pure silica, or glassmaking sand. However, silicon dioxide is supplied to glazes not only by quartz but also as a constituent of feldspar, kaolin and clays.

FELDSPAR

Feldspars are the second most important material used in most glazes. According to alkaline content (that is, K_2O and Na_2O) they are classed as **sodium feldspars** (albite), **potassium feldspars** (orthoclase and microline) and **calcareous feldspars** (anorthite). Pure feldspars practically do not exist in nature, since as a rule they contain various percentages of K_2O and Na_2O. Sodium feldspars are those whose total alkaline content is made up of at least 80 per cent Na_2O, while potassium feldspars should have at least 75 per cent K_2O of the total alkaline content. Depending on the proportions of Na_2O and K_2O, feldspars are generally designated as sodium-potassium or potassium-sodium. The alkaline content is very important in coloured glazes, since Na_2O used instead of K_2O or vice versa could totally change the colour.

Feldspars are obtained from rocks like granite or pegmatite. These supply not only the required alkaline constituents but also aluminium oxide (alumina), silicon dioxide (silica) and other components; the content of pigment oxides should not exceed two per cent. Glaze feldspar should have at least 13 per cent alkaline content. In hard glazes feldspar acts as a flux, and in glazes fired at lower temperatures it is used to increase the melting point.

KAOLIN

Its purity and whiteness make kaolin a good source of alumina and silica. It gives glazes strength and hardness. Raw kaolin prevents flocculation of glaze solutions and improves adhesion to the body during glazing. However, if too much raw kaolin is used, the glaze will peel during drying.

27
Chalice with base
Kurt Spurey, Austria, 1983
Porcelain, white base with transparent glaze, brown *temmoku* chalice; electrically fired at 1320 °C
Height 21 cm, diameter 21 cm
Private collection

28
Landscape
Johny Rolf, Netherlands, 1982
Stoneware, ochre body, decorated with white, black,
green and ferruginous slip; engraved lines rubbed
with black-brown oxides; electrically fired at 1260 °C
Height 32 cm
Private collection

Calcinated kaolin reduces the glaze shrinkage. Only top grade kaolins are used for glazes, that is those containing at least 38 per cent aluminium oxide and less than 1.2 per cent pigment oxides.

CALCAREOUS COMPOUNDS

Calcium monoxide is an important flux for temperatures exceeding 1100 °C. It gives glazes lustre as well as mechanical stability. However, the most frequently used material is calcium carbonate $CaCO_3$ supplied as floated whiting, ground limestone or ground marble. In glazes fired below 1100 °C calcium carbonate acts rather as a matting agent.

Calcium oxide is also supplied to glazes with other calcareous compounds, for example: **wollastonite**, calcium silicate $CaSiO_3$, which reduces the danger of cracking and increases resistance against abrupt temperature changes;

and **dolomite**, calcium magnesium carbonate $CaCO_3 . MgCO_3$.

MAGNESIUM COMPOUNDS

Magnesium oxide MgO produces glazes that are harder and higher-melting than those produced by calcium monoxide.

Whenever the glaze should contain both the calcium and magnesium oxide, dolomite ($CaCO_3 . MgCO_3$) is used to advantage. Dolomite increases whiteness and lustre. Other materials used as a source of magnesium include **magnesite** (magnesium carbonate $MgCO_3$) and burnt magnesia (magnesium oxide MgO).

LEAD COMPOUNDS

Lead oxide is historically the oldest flux used for low-melting (soft) glazes. Originally it used to be obtained from **galena** (lead sulphide PbS). Galena was fired in an oxidizing atmosphere and with a strong updraft to remove sulphur dioxide produced in this way. Period glazes have characteristic lustre produced by admixtures of other metals with which galena is always contaminated.

Today, **minium** is used instead because of its purity. Minium (red lead Pb_3O_4) is a heavy, fire-red powder produced by roasting lead oxide in a stream of air. Mixed with silica, it gives a transparent, slightly yellowish glaze.

Lead carbonate [white lead $2PbCO_3$. $Pb(OH)_2$] is a light white powder. Although chemically very pure, it is not used much for glazes since it can be inhaled easily and is highly toxic.

Generally speaking, lead compounds are extremely toxic and cause chronic poisoning. Lead frits are therefore preferred, because they are less soluble. Lead frits are essentially lead silicates produced by melting lead with silica.

Lead glazes are low-melting, glossy, spread and coat well and stain pigment oxides.

BORON COMPOUNDS

Boric glazes are not toxic and are characterized by a low melting point, considerable hardness and high lustre. They combine well with colorants, producing a rich scale of fine colour schades. Boron oxide partially replaces silica.

The most commonly used material is **boric acid** H_3BO_3, marketed as white crystals of pearly lustre, or **borax** (crystallized sodium tetraborate $Na_2B_4O_7$. $10H_2O$) or **burnt borax**, a white powder. Both boric acid and borax dissolve easily in water and are therefore used as borosilicates or frits.

Natural boron-bearing minerals which do not have to be fritted and used commonly in the USA include **colemanite** ($2CaO$. $3B_2O_3$. $5H_2O$), mined in Nevada and California, and **Gerstley borate**, a similar mineral containing soda, likewise mined in California.

SODIUM COMPOUNDS

Sodium oxide is needed for certain colour shades. Sodium glazes are transparent, spread well into a thin film, but are prone to cracking (crazing). This is sometimes used to advantage when making the so-called **crackle glazes** in which the content of Na_2O is increased while silica is proportionately reduced.

Sodium oxide is added to glazes as crystallic soda Na_2CO_3 . $10H_2O$ or as calcinated soda Na_2CO_3, which is better since it is anhydrous. As these materials are soluble in water, they must be fritted. Other very good sodium-bearing materials for glazes include sodium and sodium-potassium feldspars and especially **nepheline syenite** K_2O . $3Na_2O$. $4Al_2O_3$. $9SiO_2$.

Sodium chloride (rock salt NaCl) is a material used specifically for salt glazes. It is unsuitable for regular glazes since it does not produce glass in combination with silica.

POTASSIUM COMPOUNDS

Potassium oxide has a slightly lower fluxing effect than soda, but makes the tones of coloured glazes richer and sparkling.

Potash (potassium carbonate K_2CO_3) is manufactured mainly from vegetable ash and molasses, but is also produced by inorganic processes. It is highly hygroscopic.

Potassium nitrate KNO_3 is a manmade product. It is a very good oxidizing agent facilitating the melting of frits.

Raw glazes receive potassium oxide from potassium feldspars. **Cornish stone** is widely used in England and **plastic vitrox**, mined in California, is commonly used in the USA.

BARIUM COMPOUNDS

Barium monoxide BaO is added to glazes in small quantities in combination with other fluxes whose properties are improved by this oxide. It is supplied with **barium carbonate** $BaCO_3$ in the form of the mineral **witherite**, but is also produced industrially as a water-soluble toxic powder.

TIN COMPOUNDS

Stannic oxide SnO_2 is used as a white opacifier for opaque glazes. An addidion of 10-15 per cent of tin dioxide will turn a transparent glaze opaque.

Tin is also used for colouring of glazes. Combined with chromium it is used to produce a pink red, while combined with copper it produces the reduction glaze 'bull's blood'. It is found in nature as the mineral **cassiterite** but is also industrially made by roasting tin in air and marketed as the so-called **tin ash.**

ZINC COMPOUNDS

Zinc oxide ZnO plays several roles in ceramics.

Depending on the formula of the basic glaze and quantity it functions either as a flux, a matting agent, is used for fine shading of colours in an oxidizing atmosphere and serves also as a constituent of crystalline glazes.

Zinc oxide is manufactured by roasting zinc in a stream of air and marketed as a white powder known as **zinc white**.

ZIRCONIUM COMPOUNDS

Zirconium dioxide ZrO_2 ranks among intensive opacifiers of soft glazes. It is a white powder insoluble in water. For high-melting glazes zircosilicates are used instead ($ZrSO_4$), or fritted zirconia in combination with other oxides (SiO_2, ZnO, CaO, etc.). **Zircopax** is a trade name of a commercial composition of 64.88 per cent zirconium dioxide, 0.22 per cent tin dioxide and 34.28 per cent silica, marketed in the USA.

LITHIUM COMPOUNDS

Recently lithium compounds have come to be used for glaze and body formulation. Lithium compounds reduce the melting point even more than sodium or potassium compounds. It is most advantageous to work with a mixture of all three.

Lithium carbonate Li_2CO_3 is a white crystalline powder, almost insoluble in water. It is manufactured from lithium-bearing minerals, but some natural minerals like **lepidolite** $LiF . KF . Al_2O_3 . 3SiO_2$ or **spodumene** $Li_2O . Al_2O_3 . 4SiO_2$ are used more frequently.

FLUORINE COMPOUNDS

Calcium difluoride CaF_2, found in nature as the mineral **fluorite** (fluorspar), sometimes replaces feldspar as a flux, since it melts at 800 °C.

Sodium hexafluoroaluminate Na_3SiF_6, mined as **cryolite** in Greenland, has an even lower melting point than fluorspar.

Sodium hexafluorosilicate Na_2SiF_6 is a white, toxic crystallic powder. It is also used as a flux. More often, however, it is added as a chemically pure, manmade **cryolite**.

Pigment oxides dissolve in fluorine-bearing glazes in exquisite colour tones. For instance, when combined with copper oxide, fluorine produces a beautiful turquoise.

PHOSPHOROUS COMPOUNDS

Calcium phosphate is used either in the form of the mineral **phosphorite**, or as chemically pure synthetic phosphate. Other materials include **bone ash** containing approximately 85 per cent calcium carbonate. Bone ash is the oldest known opacifier producing an interesting opalescent lustre. It was used mainly in stoneware glazes of the Chinese type (Chün, Sung dynasty). Bone ash is a major ingredient of bone china formulas (see page 40).

Other metallic compounds are usually substances which are used to colour glazes. Most will dissolve in the glaze during melting, forming coloured silicates. However, the resulting colour does not depend on the colorant and its quantity but on the formula of the basic glaze and is influenced by reduction and oxidation.

COBALT COMPOUNDS

Cobalt colours rank among the oldest in use and also the most popular. They are rich and withstand even very high temperatures of hard porcelain firing. The most important cobalt compounds include:

Cobalt monoxide CoO, prepared by roasting of cobalt-bearing ores. It is extremely hard, grinds with difficulty and dissolves poorly in glazes.

Cobalt carbonate $CoCO_3$, a blueblack powder, insoluble in water. It is very popular among potters because it dissolves easily in glazes.

Thénard's blue $CoO . (Al_2O_3)_n$, a compound of cobalt and aluminium, and **Rinman's green** $CoO . ZnO$, a compound of cobalt and zinc, are excellent underglaze pigments.

Royal blue (blueing) is a finely ground glass produced by melting cobalt monoxide, potash and silica. In literature on pottery it is often termed **enamel**.

Cobalt dichloride $CoCl_2 . 6H_2O$ forms red crystals, while **cobaltous nitrate** $Co(NO_3)_2 . 6H_2O$ forms red crystals which easily absorb moisture and disintegrate. The two compounds are used for underglaze colouring salts.

Cobalt compounds for ceramic use are marketed under the following designations:

FFKO	CoO	with approx.	70 per cent	Co
RKO	C_2O_3		78	Co
FKO	Co_3O_4		72	Co
KOH	$CoCO_3$		50	Co
PKO	$Co_3(PO_4)_2$		30	Co

29
Column
Václav Šerák,
Czechoslovakia, 1982
Black oxide of manganese
body, white semi-matt
opalescent glaze;
electrically fired at
1100 °C
Height 40 cm
Exhibition of Ceramics,
Bechyně, Czechoslovakia

Cobalt compounds produce a rich blue colour, and combined with other compounds produce purple, green and black.

COPPER COMPOUNDS

The most frequently used copper compounds include:

Cupric oxide CuO, a black powder insoluble in water and manufactured by roasting copper in a stream of air. Added to alkaline glazes it produces a blue colour (**Egyptian blue**), while lead and boron-bearing alkaline glazes turn turquoise. Lead and boron glazes in combination with copper produce shades from greyish green to green.

Cuprous oxide (cuprite Cu_2O) is a red powder, insoluble in water.

Other commonly used copper compounds are **cupric carbonate** $2CuCO_3 . Cu(OH)_2$ forming blue crystals, and **cuprous sulphide** Cu_2S, a dark grey, shiny powder.

If used in an oxidizing atmosphere, copper compounds produce green and turquoise colours; when fired in a reducing atmosphere, they turn the glaze dark red. The Chinese red known as *sang de boeuf* (bull's blood) is a reduction glaze containing copper. Combined with titanium or lithium, copper produces blue colours.

CHROMIUM COMPOUNDS

Chromium compounds turn alkaline glazes rich green even at high temperatures.

Chromic oxide (chrome green Cr_2O_3) is a dark green, amorphous powder, insoluble in water. It is made by heating potassium dichromate with sulphur. Chrome green is the most commonly used substance for greens of various hues. Combined with tin oxide and calcium oxide it produces pink red in an oxidizing atmosphere.

Potassium dichromate $K_2Cr_2O_7$ is an orange crystallic powder soluble in water. The compound is toxic and is used in combination with other substances to yield pink reds.

Neutral lead chromate (chrome yellow $PbCrO_4$) and **hydroxide lead chromate** (chrome red $2PbO . PbCrO_4$) produce, depending on the composition of the basic glaze, colours ranging from yellow to coral red, although they function only at lower temperatures.

Ferric chromate [siderochromite $Fe_2(CrO_4)_3$] stains brown to black.

Other yellow pigments for temperatures up to 1040 °C include **barium yellow** $BaCrO_4$ and **lemon yellow** $PbCrO_4$.

Chromium trichloride $CrCl_3$ and **chromic nitrate** $Cr(NO_3)_3 . 9H_2O$ are used mainly for the preparation of underglaze colouring salts which give the body a green colour.

IRON COMPOUNDS

These represent the most common colours both for low and high temperatures. In an oxidizing atmosphere they colour the glaze with a range of colours from yellow to reddish brown to brick red, but when used in a reducing atmosphere, they turn glazes bluish grey to dark grey. Reduction green (celadon) glazes also contain iron. Glazes supersaturated with ferric oxide produce **aventurine** crystals. Likewise a presence of cobalt, manganese and chromium oxides affect the glaze coloration.

Ferric oxide (colcothar Fe_2O_3) is found as the mineral **hematite.** It is a reddish brown to black powder insoluble in water.

Ferric hydroxide $Fe(OH)_3$ is contained in various mineral pigments, e.g. ochre.

Ferric chloride $FeCl_3$ and **ferric nitrate** $Fe(NO_3)_3 . 9H_2O$ are used mainly for the formulation of colouring solutions used for underglaze decoration.

Ferroferric oxide (scale Fe_3O_4) is unsuitable for fine coloration. When 0.1-0.5 per cent of this oxide is used in a glaze, the latter will be slightly frosted with spots.

Iron-bearing primary and secondary clays containing a high percentage of ferric compounds are used as a main constituent of slip glazes.

MANGANESE COMPOUNDS

According to the formula of the basic glaze, firing temperature and kiln atmosphere, these compounds produce black, also brown, yellow and purple/violet.

Manganese dioxide (black oxide of manganese MnO_2) is a black powder insoluble in water used for colouring glazes.

Trimanganese tetroxide Mn_3O_4 forms black crystals insoluble in water.

Manganese dichloride $MnCl_2$ forms pink crystals soluble in water.

Some potters also use manganese-bearing clays for their slip glazes.

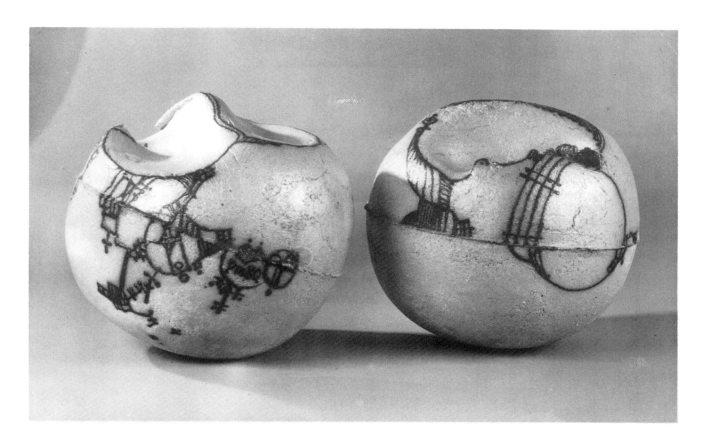

30
The Earth
Peteris Martinsons, Lithuania, USSR, 1980
Stoneware body with fireclay, thin yellow glaze,
drawing in black slip and red reduction glaze;
wood fired, biscuit at 1200 °C, glaze at 1090 °C under
reducing conditions
Diameter 40 cm
Private collection

NICKEL COMPOUNDS

Nickel compounds produce a wide range of greys and blues and even black. Depending on the formula of the glaze, they can also turn the latter green, red, purple and brown. Nickel compounds are also suitable for fine shading of colours (for example, 2 per cent cobalt with 0.2 per cent nickel will produce the Delft blue).

Nickel oxide NiO, the so-called grey-green nickel oxide, is a powder with a colour ranging from green to black.

Dinickel trioxide Ni_2O_3, the so-called black nickel oxide, is a powder of a dark grey colour.

Nickel hydroxide $Ni(OH)_2$, the so-called green nickel oxide, is a powder of apple-green colour.

Nickel carbonate $NiCO_3$ comprises pale green crystals insoluble in water.

Nickel dichloride $NiCl_2.6H_2O$ and **nickel nitrate** $Ni(NO_3).6H_2O$ are yellow, strongly hygroscopic powders used for underglaze colouring salts. These compounds produce a grey colour.

URANIUM COMPOUNDS

These substances are extremely expensive and even unavailable in some countries because they are used in the nuclear industry. Other countries have banned their use because they are dangerous to human health. In oxidizing atmospheres up to 1000 °C they turn glazes into beautiful uranium yellows and reds, but when used in a reducing atmosphere and at higher temperatures, they produce colours ranging from grey to black.

The most frequently used uranium compounds include:

Uranium dioxide (the so-called black oxide UO_2), a dark brown powder.

Uranium trioxide (the so-called brown oxide UO_3), a yellow-brown powder.

Sodium diuranate (uranium yellow $Na_2U_2O_7$), a yellow powder.

Uranyl nitrate $UO_2(NO_3)_2.6H_2O$, yellow hygroscopic crystals used for underglaze salts colouring the body yellow-brown in an oxidizing atmosphere and greyish black in a reducing atmosphere.

ANTIMONY COMPOUNDS

Antimony compounds stain yellow when used in lead glazes. A mixture of 1 part Sb_2O_3 and 9 parts ZnO produces the antimony blue. They are also used as opacifiers replacing stannic oxide.

Antimony trioxide Sb_2O_3, a white crystalline powder.

Potassium antimonate $K_2O . Sb_2O_3$.

Lead antimonate $Pb_3(SbO_4)_2$, or Naples yellow.

TITANIUM COMPOUNDS

Titanium is an excellent opacifier. When pure, it colours white, but if contaminated with iron, it produces a yellow colour. Used in a reducing atmosphere in combination with other admixtures, it colours blue and red.

Titanium dioxide TiO_2 is a crystalline or amorphous powder of white colour. It is found in nature as the mineral **rutile** which, however, is always contaminated with iron. It is one of the major raw materials for the preparation of crystalline glazes.

SILVER COMPOUNDS

Silver compounds are used as yellow pigments, as burnish silver and as an ingredient for lustre glazes. Silver comes in various compounds such as **silver chloride** AgCl and
silver oxide Ag_2O, a dark brown powder insoluble in water.

GOLD COMPOUNDS

Finely dispersed gold turns glazes various shades of purple. It is also used for surface decoration as **dull** and **bright gold**.

Gold is used in glazes in the form of **metallic gold** or as **auric chloride** $AuCl_3$, brownish yellow crystals, soluble in water and prepared by dissolving gold in **aqua regia.**

CADMIUM COMPOUNDS

Cadmium sulphide is marketed as a yellow powder known as cadmium yellow and producing colours from sulphur yellow to yellow-orange.

SELENIUM COMPOUNDS

Selenium Se is used as a metal (black and red).

Sodium selenite (white selenium Na_2SeO_3).

Barium selenite $BaSeO_3$ stains pink and a yellowish red.

A combination of selenium and cadmium sulphide produces exquisite selenium reds, albeit suitable only for low temperatures and a purely oxidizing atmosphere.

31
Cyclade
Edouard Chappalaz, Switzerland, 1984
Stoneware, white matt glaze with precipitations;
electrically fired at 1280 °C in a reducing atmosphere
55 × 53 × 22 cm
Private collection

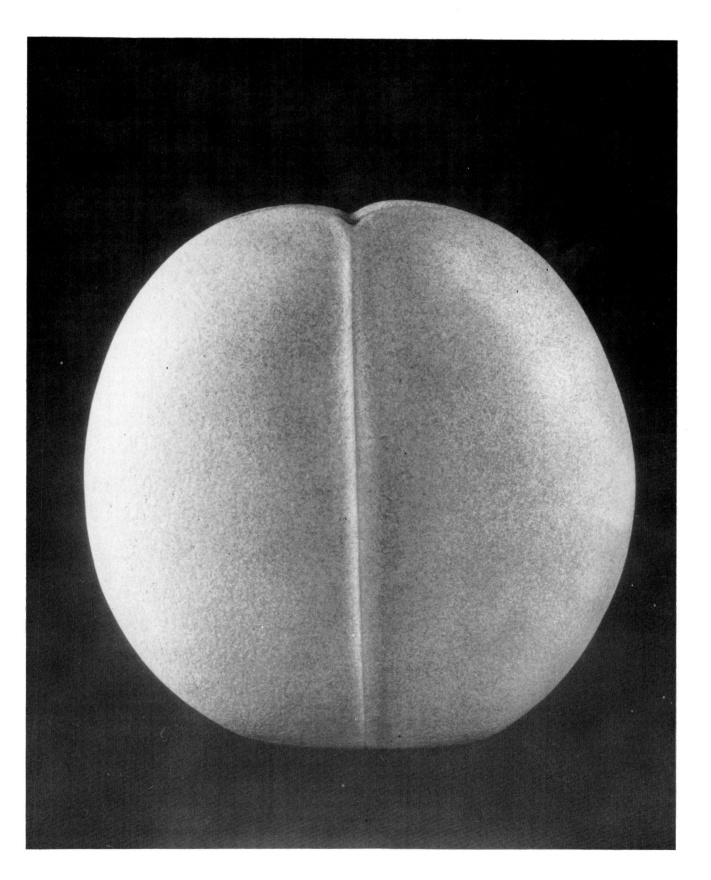

BASIC COLOURING PROPERTIES OF METALLIC OXIDES

OXIDE OF	RED	BLUE	VIOLET	YELLOW	BROWN	GREEN
CHROMIUM	Pink (with SnO and CaO); chrome red (in alkaline leadless glazes)			Chrome yellows	Various shades with Fe	In alkaline glazes
IRON	Iron red in alkaline boric glazes	With Co		In alkaline and calcareous glazes	In alkaline and calcareous glazes, also under reducing conditions	Under reduc conditions (celadon gre
COBALT	Purple	Various shades depending on quantity	Violet-blue in lead glazes			With Fe com pounds or w uranium oxi
COPPER	Chinese red under reducing conditions	Egyptian blue in alkaline glazes	Under reducing conditions			Mountain gr in lead and boron glazes turquoise in kaline leadle glazes
MANGANESE	Purplish brown in lead glazes; pink under reducing conditions	With Co	Dark violet under oxidizing conditions and in alkaline glazes	Yellow under reducing conditions	With Ti in lead glazes	
NICKLE	Purple	Delft blue with Co for low temperatures	With Zn in barium glazes	In magnesium-lead glazes	With ZnO in barium glazes	With Ti in le boron glazes
URANIUM	Orange-red in lead glazes			Lemon yellow in alkaline glazes		Under reduc conditions; under oxidi conditions w Co
ANTIMONY		Antimony blue with Sn		Naples yellow with Pb		
TITANIUM	Under reducing conditions with Zr	Reduction titanium blue	Under reducing conditions with Be or Zr	Titanium yellow with Fe and Zn		With Co or
SELENIUM	For low temperatures					
CADMIUM				Sulphur yellow to yellow-orange		
GOLD	Purples Carmines		Purplish violet			
SILVER				Straw yellow		

GREY	BLACK	NOTE
In alkaline glazes with Zn	With Fe, Mn, Co	Used in 2-5%. Withstands high temperatures
With Mn, Co, Cr	With Cr and other oxides; also under reducing conditions	Best proportion 5-10%; under 5% colours pale; above 10% produces aventurine glaze
Greyish blue with Ni or rutile	With Fe compounds or with uranium oxide	Even very small percentage will colour (that is, $^1/_2$-4%); withstands very high temperatures
		Best proportion 1-6%. At higher percentages glaze assumes metallic appearance and melting point reduces
With Fe or Ni	Metallic black with Cu and Co	Best proportion 5-10%; for lower temperatures only
Grey-blue with Co		Even small quantity (0.2-1%) will colour; excellent for fine shading of all oxides; good even for high temperatures
Under reducing conditions	Under reducing conditions	Correct proportion 5-8%; for low temperatures only
		Used in 3-6%. Various shades depend on proportion of other oxides; also used as opacifier
		Good opacifier and constituent of opaque glazes
		For low temperatures only
		2-3% will suffice
		The higher the fire, the darker the shade
		Lustres produced under reducing conditions

Molecular formulae of glazes

The substances used for making glazes are inorganic materials, frequently oxides, into which the individual constituents are converted and their molecular weights thus obtained serve as a basis for the calculation of the Seger formulae.

For example, white lead is a carbonate but it is converted into lead oxide. Some materials used in glaze formulation yield several oxides; to take an example, potassium feldspar (orthoclase $K_2O . Al_2O_3 . 6SiO_2$) is composed of oxides of potassium, aluminium and silicon.

In order to be able to survey easily all constituents of a glaze and their quantities, the ingredients are listed in a molecular (or Seger) formula which has the columns listing molecules of all oxides used in the glaze.

The first two columns list oxides of univalent metals, designated universally as R_2O and bivalent metals designated as RO. The next column lists oxides of trivalent metals (R_2O_3, for example aluminium oxide Al_2O_3), while the last column lists oxides of tetravalent elements (RO_2, for example silicon dioxide SiO_2), possibly also oxides of elements with a higher valence.

The table at the top of page 54 lists oxides of those elements which are most commonly used to formulate ceramic glazes.

NOTE: An endless variety of various shades of different colours can be obtained by mixing various oxides and adjusting their proportion. To colour a transparent glaze with oxides is not simple, since most act as a flux, reducing considerably the melting point of the glaze. On the other hand, some opacifiers increase the melting point and deviations must be corrected by adding or reducing flux. To simplify work, glazes can also be coloured with ceramic pigment stains.

<table>
</table>

R_2O-RO			
PbO	lead	FeO	ferrous
ZnO	zinc	MnO	manganese
K_2O	potassium	CdO	cadmium
Na_2O	sodium	CuO	cupric
CaO	calcium	Cu_2O	cuprous
BaO	barium	CoO	cobalt
MgO	magnesium	NiO	nickel

R_2O_3		RO_2-RO_3	
Al_2O_3	aluminium	SiO_2	silicon
B_2O_3	boron	TiO_2	titanium
Fe_2O_3	ferric	SnO_2	stannic
Cr_2O_3	chromic	ZrO_2	zirconium
Sb_2O_3	antimony	UO_3	uranium
Mn_2O_3	dimanganese	MoO_3	molybdenum

To compare different formulae, the procedure is that the sum of the first column, that is fluxes, always equals one. The figures, however, show merely the proportion of molecules but the formula still remains to be converted into a weight recipe (the so-called formula-into-recipe procedure).

By adjusting the quantity of fluxes with respect to aluminium and silicon oxides (that is, alumina and silica), or using various materials as admixtures, one can produce formulae for different temperatures and glazes of different visual/optical properties.

The following example illustrates how the proportion of molecules changes for different temperatures.

At the lowest temperatures, that is, 600-800 °C, it is possible to use only lead oxide as flux. Note that the R_2O_3 column is missing:

PbO . 1.5 SiO_2

For temperatures ranging from 800 to 860 °C the formula is as follows:

PbO . 0.05 Al_2O_3 . 1.15 SiO_2

Lead oxide is the only first column constituent and a small quantity of alumina has been added.

Listed below is a formula for a fritted transparent pottery glaze for 1000 °C:

$$\left.\begin{array}{l} 0.80 \text{ PbO} \\ 0.10 \text{ K}_2\text{O} \\ 0.10 \text{ CaO} \end{array}\right\} . \ 0.10 \text{ Al}_2\text{O}_3 . \ \left\{\begin{array}{l} 1.80 \text{ SiO}_2 \end{array}\right.$$

As can be seen, small quantities of floated whiting and feldspar as flux have been added. Likewise the content of silica and alumina has increased. K_2O and CaO are supplied by feldspar in this particular glaze.

By adding 5-10 per cent stannic or zinc oxide

the glaze can be converted into a white opaque enamel:

$$\left.\begin{array}{l} 0.80 \text{ PbO} \\ 0.10 \text{ K}_2\text{O} \\ 0.10 \text{ CaO} \end{array}\right\} 0.10 \text{ Al}_2\text{O}_3 \ \left\{\begin{array}{l} 1.80 \text{ SiO}_2 \\ 0.18 \text{ SnO}_2 \end{array}\right.$$

Chinese glaze for temperatures between 1100 and 1200 °C:

$$\left.\begin{array}{l} 0.20\text{-}0.35 \text{ PbO} \\ 0.35\text{-}0.50 \text{ CaO} \\ 0.20\text{-}0.35 \\ \text{KNaO} \\ 0.00\text{-}0.10 \text{ ZnO} \end{array}\right\} \left\{\begin{array}{l} 0.20\text{-}0.35 \text{ Al}_2\text{O}_3 \\ 0.30\text{-}0.70 \text{ B}_2\text{O}_3 \end{array}\right. \left\{\begin{array}{l} 2.0\text{-}3.5 \\ \text{SiO}_2 \end{array}\right.$$

Hard feldspathic glazes for porcelain and stoneware and fired at 1450 °C:

$$\left.\begin{array}{l} 0.00\text{-}0.40 \text{ K}_2\text{O} \\ 1.00\text{-}0.50 \text{ CaO} \\ 0.00\text{-}0.40 \text{ MgO} \end{array}\right\} 0.50 \text{ Al}_2\text{O}_3 \ \left\{\begin{array}{l} 5.0\text{-}10.0 \text{ SiO}_2 \end{array}\right.$$

However, to make a glaze using a molecular formula, the latter must first be converted into a recipe, which necessitates determining the constituents and their respective quantities.

The molecular weight is a sum of weights of all atoms making up a molecule of the compound or substance in question. For example, alumina has the molecular formula Al_2O_3 and its molecular weight is:

2 atoms of Al =	2×27 =	54
3 atoms of O =	3×16 =	48
molecular weight		102

Or potassium feldspar has the molecular formula K_2O . Al_2O_3 . $6SiO_2$. Its molecular weight is calculated as follows:

2 atoms of Al =	2×27 =	54
6 atoms of Si =	6×28 =	168
2 atoms of K =	2×39 =	78
16 atoms of O =	16×16 =	256
molecular weight		556

Molecular weights of various compounds used most frequently in ceramics will be found in the table on page 59.

VII
Plate with Neptune
Urbino, Italy, 1544
Faience
Diameter 24.5 cm
Museum of Decorative Arts, Prague

55

TO19640

VIII
Tankard
Isnik, Turkey, 16th century
Porous ware, white body
decorated with slip and
colour painting under
a transparent glaze
Metalwork and lid of
European origin
Height 24.5 cm
National Gallery, Prague

IX
Star-shaped tile
Veramin, Iran, mid-13th century
Faience with lustre decoration
Diameter 31 cm
National Gallery, Prague

X
Bahram Shooting a Gazelle, circular tile
Iran, 16th-17th century
Faience
Diameter 27 cm
National Gallery, Prague

CHEMICAL SYMBOL		MOLECULAR WEIGHT	MELTING POINT	USE
Ag	SILVER	107.88	960.5	Element, used for decoration
Ag_2O	Silver oxide	231.76	Decomposes	
AgCl	Silver chloride	143.34	455.0	Glaze pigment
Ag_2CO_3	Silver carbonate	275.77	218.0	Glaze and lustre pigment
Ag_2S	Silver sulphide	247.82	825.0	Glaze pigment
Al	ALUMINIUM	27.1	658.0	Element
Al_2O_3	Aluminium oxide (alumina)	101.94	2050.0	For matting glazes
$AlCl_3$	Aluminium chloride	133.5	192.6	
$Al_2F_6.6NaF$	Aluminium-sodium fluoride (cryolite)	420.0	1000.0	Glaze flux
$Al_2O_3.2SiO_2.2H_2O$	Kaolinite	258.09	1800.0	For porcelain bodies and other use
$Al_2O_3.6SiO_2.K_2O$	Potassium feldspar (orthoclase)	556.51	1200.0	Basic material for bodies and glazes
$Al_2O_3.6SiO_2.Na_2O$	Sodium feldspar (albite)	526.0	1180.0	Basic material for bodies and glazes
$Al_2O_3.2SiO_2.CaO$	Calcareous feldspar (anorthite)	278.9	1370	Basic material for bodies and glazes
$AlPO_4$	Aluminium phosphate	122.1	1500	
Au	GOLD	197.0	1064	Element, for gilding
$AuCl_3.2H_2O$	Auric chloride	339.6	Decomposes	Pigment
B	BORON	10.9	2300	Element
B_2O_3	Boron oxide	69.64	185	Flux
$B(OH)_3$	Boric acid	61.84	185	Flux
Ba	BARIUM	137.4	710	Element
$BaCl_2.2H_2O$	Barium chloride	244.3	960	Material for ceramic batches; used to check sulphuring
$BaCO_3$	Barium carbonate	197.4	795	Esp. porcelain pastes
Be	BERYLLIUM	9.1	321	Element
BeO	Beryllium oxide	25.1	2500	Special refractory
Bi	BISMUTH	209.0	269	Element
Bi_2O_3	Bismuth oxide	466.0	820	Flux in lustres
Ca	CALCIUM	40.0	800	Element
$CaCO_3$	Calcium carbonate (limestone-chalk)	100.1	Decomposes	Basic batch and glaze material
CaF_2	Calcium difluoride	78.1	1403	Flux
$Ca_3(PO_4)_2$	Calcium phosphate (bone ash)	310.0	1550	Batches, esp. porcelain and glazes
$CaSO_4.\frac{1}{2}H_2O$	Burnt plaster	145.06		For moulds
CaO	Calcium oxide	56.08	2585	Basic material for porcelain pastes
Cd	CADMIUM	112.4	321	Element
CdS	Cadmium sulphide	144.5	1750	Glaze pigment
Ce	CERIUM	140.3	623	Element
CeO_2	Ceric oxide	172.3	2600	Glaze pigment; opacifier
Co	COBALT	59.0	1490	Element
CoO	Cobalt oxide	75.0	1935	Pigment
$CoCO_3$	Cobalt carbonate	119.0	Decomposes	Pigment
$CoCl_2$	Cobalt chloride	129.85	735	Pigment
$CoCl_2.6H_2O$	Crystallic cobalt chloride	238.0	Dehydrates	Pigment
$Co(NO_3)_2.6H_2O$	Crystallic cobalt nitrate	291.05	Dehydrates	Pigment
Co_2O_3	Cobalt trioxide	165.9	Decomposes	Pigment
$CoSO_4.7H_2O$	Crystallic cobalt sulphate	281.2	Dehydrates	Pigment
$Co_3(PO_4)_2.8H_2O$	Cobalt phosphate	511.2		Pigment

Cr	CHROMIUM	52.0	1805	Element
Cr_2O_3	Chromium trioxide	152.2	2257	Pigment
Cu	COPPER	63.6	1064	Element
$CuCO_3.Cu(OH)_2$	Basic copper carbonate	221.17	Decomposes	Pigment
Cu_2O	Cuprous oxide	143.14	1235	Pigment
CuO	Cupric oxide	79.57	Decomposes	Pigment
Cu_2S	Copper sulphide	159.20	1100	Pigment
Fe	IRON	56.0	1500	Element
Fe_2O_3	Ferric oxide	160.0	1565	Pigment (brownstone) and flux
Fe_3O_4	Ferroferric oxide (scale)	231.52	1550	Pigment and flux
$Fe(OH)_3$	Iron hydroxide	213.7		Pigment and flux
$Fe_2(SO_4)_3.9H_2O$	Crystalline iron sulphate	562.0	Dehydrates	Pigment and flux
$Fe_2(CrO_4)_3$	Iron chromate (siderochromite)	460.0		Pigment
H_2	HYDROGEN	2.0	259.4	Element
H_2O	Water	18.02		Wide use
K	POTASSIUM	39.1	62.5	Element
$K_2Cr_2O_7$	Potassium dichromate	294.2	400.0	Pigment
K_2CrO_4	Potassium chromate	194.2	980.0	Pigment
K_2CO_3	Potassium carbonate (potash)	138.2	878.0	Flux
KNO_3	Potassium nitrate	101.1	339.0	Flux
$KMnO_4$	Potassium permanganate	158.0	Decomposes	Pigment
K_2SO_4	Potassium sulphate	174.4	1078.0	Flux
$K_2U_2O_7$	Potassium uranate	666.0		Pigment
Li	LITHIUM	6.9	180.0	Element
Li_2CO_3	Lithium carbonate	73.9	700.0	Flux
Mg	MAGNESIUM	24.4	650	Element
$MgCl_2.6H_2O$	Crystalline magnesium chloride	203.3	106	Material for Sorel enamel
$MgCO_3$	Magnesium carbonate	84.3	Decomposes	Material for refractories
MgO	Magnesium oxide	40.3	2000	Constituent of refractories
Mn	MANGANESE	54.9	1250	Element
MnO_2	Manganese dioxide	87.0	Decomposes	Pigment
$MnCl_2$	Manganese chloride	125.84	650	Pigment
$MnCO_3$	Manganese carbonate	114.9	Decomposes	Pigment
Mn_3O_4	Manganese tetroxide	228.9	1705	Pigment
Na	SODIUM	23.0	98	Element
$NaCO_3$	Sodium carbonate (calcined soda)	106.0	849	Chief material for glazes
$NaCO_3.10H_2O$	Crystalline sodium carbonate	286.0	Dehydrates	Glaze constituent
NaCl	Sodium chloride (rock salt)	58.45	800	Glaze constituent
$NaHCO_3$	Sodium hydrogen carbonate (cooking soda)	84.01	Decomposes	
$NaNO_3$	Sodium nitrate	85.0	310	
Na_2SiO_3	Sodium silicate (waterglass)	272.2	1000	
$Na_2B_4O_7.10H_2O$	Sodium tetraborate (borax)	382.2	741	Flux
$Na_2U_2O_7$	Sodium uranate	635.0	Decomposes	Pigment
Ni	NICKEL	58.7	1450	Element
Ni_2O_3	Dinickel trioxide	165.4	1870	Pigment
NiO	Nickel oxide	74.7	1990	Pigment
$NiSO_4.7H_2O$	Crystalline nickel sulphate	280.9	Decomposes	Pigment
Pb	LEAD	207.3	327.0	Element
$2PbCO_3.Pb(OH)_2$	Basic lead carbonate (white lead)	775.6	Decomposes	Flux
PbO	Lead oxide (litharge)	223.21	350	Flux
Pb_3O_4	Trilead tetroxide (red lead, red oxide)	685.6	Decomposes	Flux
$PbCrO_4$	Lead chromate	323.22	844	Flux
Pt	PLATINUM	195.2	1751	Element, used for decoration

Sb	ANTIMONY	6.62	630.5	Element
Sb_2O_3	Antimony trioxide	291.52	656.0	Pigment and opacifier
Se	SELENIUM	48.0	220	Element
Si	SILICON	28.3	1480	Element
SiC	Silicon carbide	40.36	2000	Batch constituent
SiO_2	Silicon dioxide (silica)	60.02	1670	Batch and glaze constituent
Sn	TIN	118.7	332	Element
SnO_2	Tin oxide	150.7	1127	Glaze constituent
Ti	TITANIUM	48.1	1850	Element
TiO_2	Titanium dioxide (contained in rutile)	80.01	1560	Pigment
U	URANIUM	238.2	800	Element
UO_2	Uranium dioxide	270.0	2176	Pigment
UO_3	Uranium trioxide	286.07	Decomposes	Pigment
W	TUNGSTEN	183.92	3400	Element
$WO_3.H_2O$	Wolframic (tungstic) acid	250.0		Constituent of crystalline glazes
Zn	ZINC	65.4	419	Element
ZnO	Zinc oxide	81.4	2000	Used for fine shading of colours
Zr	ZIRCONIUM	90.6	220	Element
ZrO_2	Zirconium dioxide (zirconia)	122.6	2250	Constituent of refractories, glaze opacifier

FORMULA-INTO-RECIPE

Let us now calculate a recipe for a glaze used for 1000 °C. Its molecular formula is as follows:

$$\left.\begin{array}{l} 0.80\ PbO \\ 0.10\ K_2O \\ 0.10\ CaO \end{array}\right\} \qquad 0.10\ Al_2O_3 \qquad \{\ 1.80\ SiO_2$$

First of all, it is necessary to know the raw materials, that is constituents, and their chemical composition. In this particular case, the following materials will be used:

Minium Pb_3O_4	mol. weight 685.6
Floated whiting CaO	100
Feldspar $Al_2O_3 . 6SiO_2 . K_2O$	556
Pure silica SiO_2	60

It is assumed that all constituents are pure.

For ease of calculation, the raw materials are entered in the following chart:

RECIPE				MOLECULAR FORMULA				
				PbO 0.80	K_2O 0.10	CaO 0.10	Al_2O_3 0.10	SiO_2 1.80
Material	Quantity of compound in formula	Molecular weight	Quantity					

The raw materials and their quantity are entered in the lefthand column of the chart, while the number of molecules used up from the molecular formula in this way is entered in the right-hand columns.

The first constituent, that is PbO, is obtained from red lead (minium) Pb_3O_4. However, since one molecule of red lead produces three molecules of PbO, to obtain one molecule of PbO only one third of the red lead is required. As the molecular weight of Pb_3O_4 equals 685.6, one third equals $\frac{685.6}{3}$, that is 229. Since the required quantity is 0.80, it is necessary to multiply 229 by 0.80 which equals 183.20. The first line of the chart will then read:

Material	Quantity of compound in formula	Molecular weight	Quantity	PbO 0.80	K_2O 0.10	CaO 0.10	Al_2O_3 0.10	SiO_2 1.80
Red lead	$\frac{685.6}{3} \times 0.80$	183.2		0.80 / 0.00				

61

The PbO column reads 0.80 which means that the required quantity of lead has been obtained.

Floated whiting (CaO, molecular weight 100) will yield the required quantity of CaO. The chart will read as follows:

Material	Quantity of compound in formula	Molecular weight	Quantity	PbO 0.80	K₂O 0.10	CaO 0.10	Al₂O₃ 0.10	SiO₂ 1.80
Red lead	$\frac{685.6}{3} \times 0.80$	183.2	$\frac{0.80}{0.00}$					
Whiting	100×0.10	10.0				$\frac{0.10}{0.80}$		

K_2O will be obtained from feldspar ($Al_2O_3 \cdot 6SiO_2 \cdot K_2O$, molecular weight 556). The entry in the third line of the chart will be then as follows: $556 \times 0.10 = 55.6$. However, as feldspar also contains aluminium and silicon it is necessary to add also $0.1 \times 1 = 0.1 \; Al_2O_3$ and $0.1 \times 6 = 0.6 \; SiO_2$. The chart will now read:

Material	Quantity of compound in formula	Molecular weight	Quantity	PbO 0.80	K₂O 0.10	CaO 0.10	Al₂O₃ 0.10	SiO₂ 1.80
Red lead	$\frac{685.6}{3} \times 0.80$	183.2	$\frac{0.80}{0.00}$					
Whiting	100×0.10	10.00				$\frac{0.10}{0.00}$		
Feldspar	556×0.10	55.6			$\frac{0.10}{0.00}$		$\frac{0.10}{0.00}$	$\frac{0.60}{1.20}$

Feldspar has now met the requirements for K_2O and Al_2O_3. Only 1.20 of silica SiO_2 is needed now. This is supplied with silica sand SiO_2 (molecular weight 60) and the chart will read:

Material	Quantity of compound in formula	Molecular weight	Quantity	PbO 0.80	K₂O 0.10	CaO 0.10	Al₂O₃ 0.10	SiO₂ 1.80
Red lead	$\frac{685.6}{3} \times 0.80$	183.2	$\frac{0.80}{0.00}$					
Whiting	100×0.10	10.0				$\frac{0.10}{0.00}$		
Feldspar	556×0.10	55.6			$\frac{0.10}{0.00}$		$\frac{0.10}{0.00}$	$\frac{0.60}{1.20}$
Silica	60×1.20	72.0						$\frac{1.20}{0.00}$

The proportional recipe of the glaze is then:

Red lead	183.20 parts by weight, that is	57.1 %
Whiting	10.00	3.1 %
Feldspar	55.60	17.4 %
Silica	72.00	22.4 %
Total	320.80 parts by weight, that is	100.0 %

A reverse method can be used to convert a recipe into a molecular formula. Using the same molecular formula one can produce different recipes, depending on the materials used, but the resulting glazes may differ considerably. This is also why it is so difficult to imitate such glazes as the Chinese celadon or *sang de boeuf*, even though their chemical analysis is known. The main reason is that the materials used for the formulation of these glazes remain unknown.

Making glazes

All required materials are weighed precisely according to the recipe and mixed thoroughly and sometimes ground.

Raw glazes are made from materials insoluble in water and, therefore, they need not be fritted. Fritted glazes are composed of about 80 per cent frit and 20 per cent other admixtures. Frit is a glassy, that is vitrified, substance (silicate) melted from water-soluble materials (for example, soda, borax, etc.) or toxic substances (lead, barium). When melted with silica, and possible other materials, the water-soluble constituents become insoluble whilst toxic substances less toxic.

Frits are melted in a crucible (fig. 12). The molten glaze is let out in a stream into a tank of cold water. Due to rapid cooling, the material disintegrates into tiny fragments which are then easily ground. Industrially manufactured glazes are melted continuously in large tank furnaces.

The frit is then milled together with pigments and other admixtures in a jar mill. For studio work, an ideal solution is a small jar mill rotating on two rollers, one being driven by a small electric motor (fig. 13).

The milling time is crucial since if the glaze is ground too finely or too coarsely, glazing may be a problem (see section on glaze flaws, page 69).

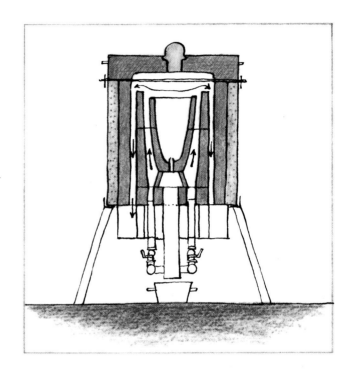

Fig. 12 Schematic diagram of a fritting crucible

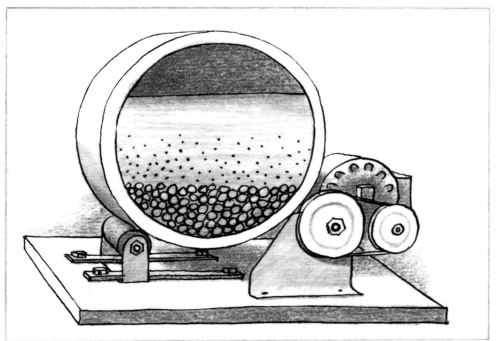

Fig. 13 Schematic diagram of a jar mill filled to one-third with pebbles and one-third with material to be ground

Glazing

The dry powder glaze is mixed with water to form a slip glaze. Using a little water, a thick, well-mixed paste is prepared and then thinned to the required consistency. Industrially manufactured glazes usually mix very well and, therefore, it usually suffices to strain them through a fine-mesh sieve, termed **lawn** by potters. However, some glazes, especially those applied by spraying, must first be ground well in a jar mill or with a mortar and pestle to prevent clogging of the spray gun nozzle.

The thickness of slip glazes usually differs according to use. A thick, porous body which absorbs water quickly requires a glaze much thinner than a dense, thin-walled or less porous body which would not be able to absorb the water. Factories working with uniform bodies and glazes for long periods of time usually check the slip density with density meters. In studio use, the consistency of glazes can be checked using a potsherd dipped in the slip and then scratched to determine the thickness of the glaze. Some glazes must be applied thickly, others must be overlayed in thin coats. The correct thickness of the glaze layer is determined by comparative glaze trials. Generally speaking, the glaze should be as thick as cream and the correct layer thickness should be about 1.5-2 mm.

32
Oval dish
Jean-Claude de Crousaz, Switzerland, 1985
Stoneware with feldspathic glaze, painting on raw glaze; gas-fired at 1300 °C in a reducing atmosphere
40 × 25 cm
Private collection

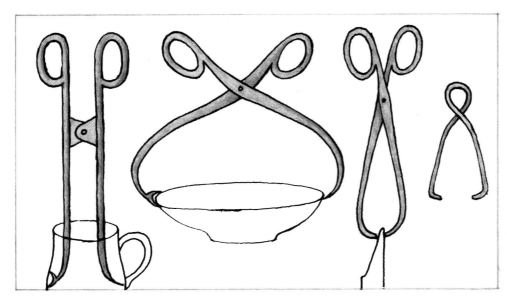

Fig. 14   Glazing tongs

Fig. 15   Glazing a dish
by dipping, using tongs

The mixed glaze must not be allowed to settle in the vessel. If it becomes settled at the bottom or tends to stick to it, it is advisable to add a weak solution of acetic acid, oxalic acid or kaolin, bentonite or two to three per cent starch, dextrin, etc. Settling may be also caused by a crazed vessel which will absorb water from the glaze. Glazes are best kept in enamelled metal or plastic vessels.

If you need the glaze to adhere to the body better (for example, to facilitate painting on the glaze), a small quantity of gum arabic or dextrin may be added. However, if used too liberally, the glue will cause glaze peeling. It is usually better to prepare enough glaze to last for a few days only since the glue starts decaying after some time.

Prior to glazing, the body must be thoroughly dusted using a brush or a stream of air. Care must

be taken not to touch the body with greasy fingers, since the glaze would crawl when fired.

Bodies may be glazed by pouring, dipping, rolling and spraying, as shown in figs 15-23. The simplest method is **dipping**, that is, immersing the body in the glaze by holding it in a glazing gripper (fig. 15) which leaves only minute unglazed spots that can be easily retouched. Note that the edge which enters the glaze first remains immersed longer than the other and is therefore coated with a thicker coat of glaze. This is dis-

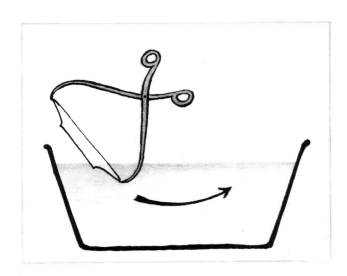

Fig. 16   Glazing a dish
by sweeping it through
glaze

65

cernible in some glazes, especially translucent coloured ones, by a slightly different colour shade. In such cases it is advisable to follow the method shown in figs 16, 17. This dish enters the glaze at one edge, leaving it by the other.

Bernard Leach suggests an interesting and quick method of glazing deeper dishes and cups. The cup is held by the bottom, dipped slowly in the glaze, then raised with a sharp jerk and dipped again (fig. 18).

To dip larger pots or objects would require too much glaze and large dipping vessels and, therefore, should be avoided in studio work. Pouring or spraying should be used instead.

Some methods of glaze **pouring** are shown in figs 19, 20. The potter rotates the jug to cover the entire body in one motion (fig. 19). Glazing of the

Fig. 17   Glazing a plate or a dish

Fig. 18   Glazing a deep cup by jerking

Fig. 19   Glazing a jug by pouring

Fig. 20   Glazing a bowl by pouring

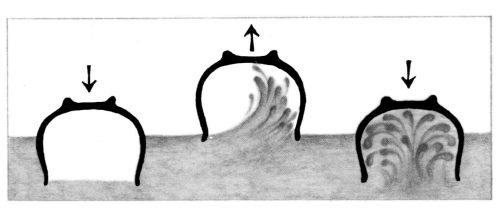

Fig. 21 Glazing insides of a pot

Fig. 22 Glazing insides of a jug — phase 1

inside surface of small pots can be seen from fig. 21. The pot is held in the right hand and filled to about one-third with the glaze. It should be kept **rolled,** then quickly upturned to pour out the glaze, rotating all the time. The method is not as complicated as it may seem; in fact, it is very quick since the whole operation takes only a few seconds. One of the main advantages of the method is that the body does not have time to absorb too much water during the operation.

Larger wares, for instance vases, are two-thirds filled with glaze and then the glaze is poured out while the body is slowly rotated to allow even coverage of the unglazed surface (figs 22, 23).

Whenever an even glaze is not required, or where glazes of different colour are used, it is best to use a brush, preferably a soft, flat bristle one. The body should be coated evenly and care must be taken not to leave any unglazed spots. If the glaze coat is too thick, it is best removed by a comb spatula and then smoothed.

Glazes can be also sprayed with a spray gun. It is a very good method, especially suitable for stu-

Fig. 23 Glazing insides of a jug — phase 2

Glaze firing

dio work, since even large bodies can be glazed using a small quantity of glaze . No large dipping tubs or bucketfuls of glaze are needed.

To prevent clogging of the gun nozzle, the glaze to be used must be carefully strained and be somewhat thinner than for other methods of application. Spraying must be done systematically, covering the entire surface evenly but avoiding spraying one place several times, otherwise the layer of glaze would be too thick in places. In fact, the thickness of the coat should be checked at short intervals by scratching the glaze. Since spraying produces fine atomized mist in the air, health protection regulations require that an exhaust system be installed to minimize hazard to human health, especially when lead glazes are being used.

Naturally, the kiln temperature must be adjusted to the melting point of the glaze. In fact, glazes do not have a sharply defined melting point as do metals, but pass from a thick liquid to a liquid paste. Glazes should not be overfired because higher temperatures would turn them more liquid and the glaze would run off, taking with it the under-glaze or on-glaze decoration. At even higher temperatures the glaze would run off completely or would be absorbed if the body happened to be porous. On the other hand, underfired glazes are rough, blistery or foamy in spots.

During the melting process the glaze enters into a chemical reaction with the body which is also partially melted. The temperature at which the clay becomes pyroplastic must, therefore, be higher than the melting point of the glaze to avoid bloating or even deformation of the body. In other words, if the clay vitrifies at 1200 °C, the glaze melting point must be lower than 1200 °C.

Another important thing which must be borne in mind is that the glaze and the body should have the same coefficient of thermal expansion, or coefficients as close as possible.

As all materials expand with heat and contract when they are cooled and since the body and the glaze usually do not have an identical coefficient of thermal expansion, cooling results in strain between the body and the glaze. This causes the two most common glazing faults, that is, crazing and peeling. Crazing results when the glaze has a higher shrinkage than the body. If it is the other way

Fig. 24 *Testing shrinkage of body and glaze:*
(a) Glaze shrinkage higher than that of the body
(b) Glaze shrinkage same as that of the body
(c) Glaze shrinkage smaller than that of the body

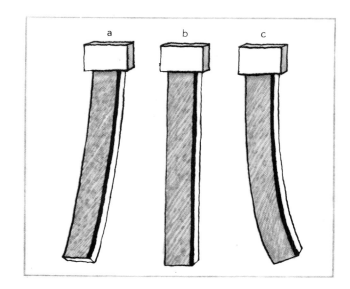

round, the glaze will peel. Prior to using a new body of glaze formula, a simple test should be performed. Thin strips are prepared from the same batch as the body and coated on one side with the glaze to be used. Then they are hung in the kiln and fired. A correct glaze will not bend the strip. If the glaze has a greater shrinkage than the body, the strip will be bent concavely on the glazed side; if the shrinkage is smaller than that of the body, the strip will be bent concavely on the unglazed side (see fig. 24).

GLAZE FLAWS AND THEIR CORRECTION

Crazing may be prevented by changing the recipe of the glaze or body. The glaze recipe may be made with less silica while increasing the proportion of boron oxide, or the glaze may be fired at a higher temperature, for example, one or two Seger cones higher. It is also possible to extend the firing time. Other possibilities include increasing CaO in relation to alkaline oxides, or increasing Al_2O_3 in alkaline glazes (either in the frit or by increasing kaolin in the slip). In lead glazes PbO may be increased while reducing CaO. However, it is easier to adjust the body formula, especially in studio practice. The proper ways are to increase silica in the body, reduce the fluxes, adjust the grain of silica used for the body or adjust the biscuit firing temperature.

Glaze peeling will be prevented by the following methods: increasing silica in the body, increasing the total fluxes in the body or increasing kaolinite in the body. Glazes can be adjusted by reducing boron in the glaze while increasing silica. Both defects, that is, crazing and peeling, can also be caused by a too finely ground glaze. Should coarser grain fail to help, the glaze-body fit can be improved by adding dextrin or gum arabic. It is also possible to try out lower or higher biscuit temperatures or to apply a thinner glaze coat. It should also be borne in mind that glazes ground too finely tend to develop flaws. Peeling may be caused by low plasticity of the clay, or by too rapid drying of glazed biscuit prior to glost-firing.

Rough glaze and blistering can be remedied by firing at a higher temperature or by reducing the melting point by adding flux. In coarsely ground glazes unmelted grains of silica cause roughness.

Crawling of the glaze is caused by greasy or dusty biscuit. It is therefore very important to dust the body well prior to glazing. Greasy wares should be refired.

Minor flaws of the glaze (especially in tin glazes) can be experienced if the body is too open. The remedy is either to use a body with finer grain or to increase calcium oxide by as much as 30 per cent.

Many defects are due to faulty glaze application. Thin slip glazes will soak the body, resulting in a poor glaze-body fit, so that the glaze will peel after drying. In addition, pot rims remain unglazed after firing.

A glaze which is too thick is impossible to apply evenly; the glaze will develop cracks even when unfired and will eventually peel. If the glaze is applied too thickly, it will run off.

Likewise under- or over-firing of biscuit may result in faulty glazing. If a body is biscuit-fired at too high a temperature, or if it is too smooth and nonporous, the glaze will adhere poorly to the surface, or will do so in a very thin layer, which will result in unglazed spots. Such biscuit should be carefully heated and glazed when warm. The water which could not be absorbed earlier will evaporate now, and a sufficiently thick glaze coat will form on the surface. On the other hand, under-fired biscuit absorbs water too rapidly from the glaze. This again may result in thick glaze, and shivering may take place.

Glaze types

TRANSPARENT GLAZES

Colourless glazes

These are basic glazes which can be turned into transparent coloured, opaque white or coloured, crackle glazes as well as run slips, etc., by adding various admixtures. The composition differs according to temperature and purpose.

Coloured glazes

Transparent colourless glazes are stained by various metal oxides which can be added to a basic glaze or mixed with other raw materials prior to fritting. Coloured and colourless translucent glazes are used especially for bodies decorated with some underglaze decoration technique. Combinations of coloured body with coloured glaze can often produce interesting results.

SLIP GLAZES

These are unfritted **feldspathic** and **argillaceous** glazes prepared from natural minerals like feldspar, quartz (silica), limestone, volcanic rocks, slip clays and some other natural materials like vegetable ashes. They are used for stoneware, hard porous wares and hard porcelain, that is, for wares fired at high temperatures (above 1250 °C).

Slip clays are characterized by fine grain, high content of iron and low melting point; some may be used directly. When washed, they form the so-called glazing slips. Brownstone stains them dark brown, iron will colour them reddish brown while marl will lend them a yellow colour. If necessary, they can be softened (that is, their melting point lowered) by adding lime, feldspar, soda or borax. They can even be used successfully on unfired (green) dried bodies.

Many recipes call for the so-called **Albany slip**, a material mined near Albany, New York. However, slip clays are found practically everywhere in the world and it is, therefore, possible to utilize your local sources.

Slip glazes have many advantages. They are cheap, can be prepared easily and are easy to work with because they have a considerable firing range. However, their colours remain rather limited; the spectrum ranges from yellow-brown to brown-red to black. This coloration is due to their iron content.

Slip glazes are often used for Asian types of stoneware and porcelain as constituents of iron

33
Vase in form of a gold dust bag
A Kyoto master, Japan, 2nd half of 17th century
Stoneware with slip glaze
Height 13.5 cm
National Gallery, Prague

34
Owl
Lubor Těhník, Czechoslovakia, 1983
Black oxide of manganese body, matt white glaze, gold; electrically fired at 1100 °C
Height 32 cm
Private collection

temmoku glazes (**hare's for**, **oil spots**, **partridge feather** and other types).

OPAQUE GLAZES

These are white or coloured glazes made opaque by various means. The opacity of a glaze is caused by the fact that light will not pass through the material due to the character of the surface or the inner structure of the glassy material. It is produced in three different ways: either light is absorbed by an opacifier dissolved in the glaze, or it is reflected from facets of crystals dispersed in the glaze, or the glaze is made impervious by finely dispersed bubbles and minute crystals.

The best opacifier is tin oxide which, however, is frequently replaced by cheaper opacifiers like zirconium oxide (zirconia), antimony dioxide or zinc oxide used in alkaline glazes. Opaque glazes are used mostly for lower firing temperatures and are typical for maiolica wares. They are usually decorated with painting into raw glaze, a technique known, for example, from Italian Renaissance maiolica, Delft faience, Habaner ware, etc.

MATT GLAZES

Matt glazes are glasses with invisible crystals produced by the melting process. A uniform crystallization lends these glazes a matt appearance and makes them velvety smooth to the touch.

Compared with glossy glazes, matt ones contain more lime, zinc oxide and clay, and less silica. Normal glazes are sometimes matted with 10-15 per cent calcium oxide or 10-50 per cent kaolin. It is very difficult to matt boron glazes in this way. Glazes can also be matted by adding 5 per cent rutile and 5 per cent zinc oxide.

Stoneware glazes can be well matted by adding ground volcanic rocks like basalt, trachyte, phonolite or pumice. Lead glazes are matted by adding talc. A very good matting agent for all types of glazes is strontium carbonate (20-40 per cent). Naturally, it is always best to do a glaze test and, if necessary, to adjust the recipe.

Depending on the matting agent used, glazes with different internal structures of the glass can be obtained. Glazes matted with kaolin have a totally different surface from those using an admixture of tin oxide or titanium dioxide. Coloured glazes produce surprisingly different colour shades if matted.

A method of glaze matting after firing is used in porcelain-making. The glaze of the fired ware is etched by a mixture of two parts concentrated hydrofluoric acid and ten parts concentrated hydrochloric acid. Two or three minutes after application the body is thoroughly rinsed. Note that rubber gloves and a breathing mask (respirator) must be worn. Hydrofluoric acid is a very dangerous substance. Burns caused by it heal poorly and leave deep scars.

Glazes may also be matted by sandblasting, a technique used in the glass industry.

RUN SLIPS

In one respect, run slips are just the opposite of matt glazes. Whilst in some cases the latter are produced from normal glazes by underfiring, it is also possible to overfire a glaze by about 80 °C to achieve a run-off effect. For example, glazes formulated for 1000 °C can be used as run slips if overfired at 1080 °C. For porcelain, leadless stoneware glazes may be used, especially to soften regular porcelain slip. Lead glazes are unsuitable, because porcelain is fired in a reducing atmosphere.

It is also possible to fire at the regular firing temperature and soften the glaze by adding 30-50 per cent low-melting frit or one to two-thirds fritted quartz and boric acid. Good results can be obtained by adding 20 per cent boric acid to the jar mill when the glaze is ground and to use it unfritted.

Run slips are either sprayed or applied in a thick coat using a brush. Several glazes of different colours or even different melting points may be used. When fired, the glazes will run one over the other, forming fantastic multi-coloured patterns. Finished fired pots can also be improved or retouched with a thick glaze containing dextrin or some other glue.

All wares decorated with run slip must be placed on kiln furniture to catch the excess run-off slip and to avoid damaging the kiln by bonding the pot to the refractory lining.

CRACKLE GLAZES

While crazing represents one of the major glazing defects of a finished pot, sometimes a fine network of hairline cracks is desirable for the decorative effect it produces. Such cracks are the result of an uneven shrinkage of the body and the glaze. The greater the shrinkage of the glaze as compared to that of the body, the greater the strain generated between the two materials and the finer the cracks. Normal glazes can be turned into crackle ones by replacing lime with feldspar.

The cracks are sometimes deliberately made more pronounced by staining using various methods. Japanese potters use regular China ink for the purpose. To obtain a greyish black colour, it is possible to use a saturated sugar solution mixed with an equal part of concentrated sulphuric acid. Porous wares must be stained very carefully to prevent the body from absorbing too much solution due to the effect of the acid. The pot is then cleaned thoroughly and heated to about 350 °C (that is, the boiling point of the acid). The acid will evaporate and sugar will carbonize. For staining pigment, salts or very finely ground underglaze colours are used. The cracks are stained, if necessary several times, depending on the ability of the body to absorb the stain, and the pigment is then fired into the body at a temperature used to fire overglaze colours. If the pot is glost-fired, traces of the first staining will appear under the glaze. When the pot cools, crackles will appear in different places, which are then stained with a different colour. The technique can also be applied to wares coated with regular uncrazed glazes. Crackles can be produced artificially by heating the pot and then sprinkling cold water on the surface. After crackle staining and refiring the coloured crackle pattern will remain coated with perfect glaze. The same effect can be achieved if a normal glaze is underfired by 80-100 °C. Crackles produced by incorrect firing are then stained and the pot is refired once again at the correct temperature.

Another technique of crackling uses slip. The pot is covered with a regular white or coloured opaque slip and overlaid with another coat of the same composition but a different colour. To achieve the required shrinkage rate, an adequate quantity of clay is added. The pot is then fired and crazing of the top glaze, which can be as much as several millimetres wide, will reveal the underglaze.

Alternatively, it is possible to fire the underglaze first and then overglaze the pot with the same glaze mixed with 25-50 parts by weight dextrin. The solution must be strained prior to use, using a fine lawn. The overglaze will craze even during the drying stage, producing a fine pattern of hairline cracks. Naturally, wares crackledecorated this way must be fired twice.

It is also good to work with a heated body and hot overglaze in the last two cases described above, since water will adhere well and not run.

CRYSTALLINE GLAZES

Crystalline glazes rank among the most effective of the so-called artwork glazes. What happens essentially is that during the cooling process crystals, resembling patterns produced by frost on windowpanes, form in the glaze.

Very beautiful effects can be achieved by adding 10-25 per cent rutile to a well-tested run slip stained by 5-6 per cent cupric oxide, 1-2 per cent uranium trioxide or 5-6 per cent manganese monoxide.

Pigment oxides or commercial stains produce rich hues, but crystalline glazes can be given fine pastel hues when used on bodies stained with solutions of colouring metal salts.

Good results will be obtained if the crystalline glaze is applied thinly on a matt underglaze or on vitrified biscuit, since the glaze absorbs fewer undesirable constituents (that is, silica and alumina) from the body as compared to normal biscuit firing. However, the glaze must contain glue and the body must be heated. The glaze must be applied several times and every coat must be left to dry before proceeding with the next one. The procedure is repeated until the desired thickness of the coat is achieved.

Large crystals are also produced by zinc oxide (10-30 per cent), especially when used in glazes poor in silica. Adding a minute quantity of vanadium, tungsten or molybdenum compounds will considerably enhance crystallization.

Crystalline glazes should usually be fired in an oxidizing atmosphere although, for example, a crystalline glaze containing vanadium will turn fire red in a slightly reducing atmosphere.

The proportion of rutile and zinc oxide must not exceed certain limits because oversaturation would produce a hard crust and rough blothes in the glaze would result.

In the glazes discussed so far the arrangement of crystals is left to chance but if crystals are desired in specific places, the method is to prepare a frit free of clay components but rich in zinc oxide and an appropriate pigment. Slivers of the melted frit are then placed into a basic, preferably zinc-bearing, glaze in the places where crystals are desired.

Also very popular are aventurine crystals formed in alkaline, leadless or low lead glazes by adding a larger quantity of ferrous oxide (which should be pure, without argillaceous admixtures). Good results will also be obtained with powdered metallic iron, pyrite or iron scale. Aventurine

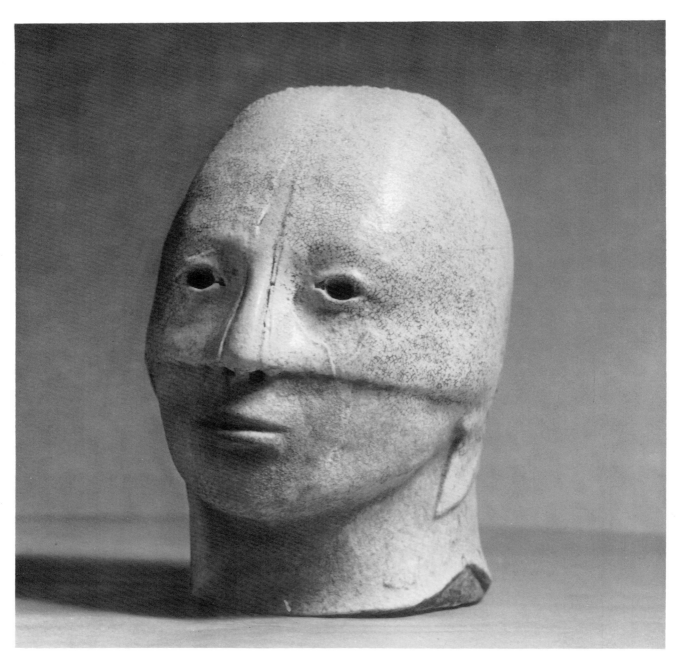

35
Green Helmeted Head
Carmen Dionyse, Belgium, 1984
Whiteware; upper part glazed with matt opalescent
white glaze, lower part with turquoise crystalline
glaze; electrically fired, biscuit at 1075 °C, glost-fired
at 1050 °C
Height 24 cm
Private collection

XI
Hexagonal Mokuzuke dish
Japan, 17th century
Glazed Oribe stoneware decorated with motifs of lake
and reeds
Diameter 22.5 cm
National Gallery, Prague

XII
Tsubo box with lid
Kutani, Japan, late 17th century
Porcelain decorated with enamels
Height 7.7 cm, diameter 19 cm
National Gallery, Prague

XIII
Wax box
Jumino shop, Karatsu, Japan, 18th century
Stoneware decorated with painting on engraved slip
under transparent feldspathic glaze
Height 25 cm, diameter 36.5 cm
National Gallery, Prague

XIV
Bowl
Vietnam (?), late 17th century
Porcelain with blue banding and stencilled symbols
under bluish transparent glaze
Diameter 26 cm
Private collection

XV
Chrysanthemum-shaped bowl
China, Ch'ing dynasty, 18th century
Porcelain with hidden *an-chua* underglaze decoration
Height 8 cm, diameter 17 cm
National Gallery, Prague

glazes require a purely oxidizing atmosphere and lime-free bodies rich in silica. Similarly, aventurine glazes may be produced by oversaturation of the glaze with chromic oxide or sodium diuranate. Unlike other crystalline glazes in which the crystals are deposited on the surface, aventurine crystals are embedded in the glaze coat.

As crystalline glazes tend to run, wares loaded inside the kiln for firing must be placed on suitable kiln furniture and separated from it by a coat of a thick mixture of kaolin and alumina.

LUSTRE GLAZES

Lustre glazes are shiny, iridescent and strongly refracting. Essentially, they are lead glazes containing 1-5 per cent oxide of silver, bismuth, vanadium, molybdenum, cobalt, copper and other metals. They are first glost-fired in an oxidizing atmosphere to the required temperature and then lustred in a strongly reducing atmosphere. Reduction should take place for about three half-hour periods at a temperature drop to about 800 °C. As reducing agents, materials producing much smoke are used, for example, naphtaline, asphalt, oxalic acid, rags soaked in oil, etc. Reduction is sometimes achieved during the first firing when the kiln cools down to the required temperature. In other cases, the wares are separately refired for reduction. Double firing is advantageous, however, because reduction can be performed in another kiln and on selected fired wares only. In fact, one should always use a separate kiln for reduction firing, since if a kiln is used for both types of firing, the effect of the previous reducing atmosphere might ruin the subsequent oxidizing firing. Electric resistance furnaces are not recommended for firing in a reducing atmosphere, because it greatly affects the life of the heating elements.

Islamic lustre faience wares used to be decorated with underglaze painting, pigments used on raw glazes as well as by overglaze painting. The secret of lustre-glazed faience was revealed by Abu-el-Khassim of Tabriz in his treatise dating from 1301. The body was composed of 10 parts silica sand, 1 part frit and 1 part white clay. The frit was melted from 105 parts silica sand and 100 parts potash. To increase plasticity an organic substance of unknown identity was added.

The fired lead-tin glaze was painted with lustre paints composed of 1 part pigment oxides and 3 parts ochre or whiting, iron oxide, etc., depending on the colour required. The paint was ground with vinegar and turpentine and the painted body was then refired to the temperature of the under-

glaze and left to cool in a reducing atmosphere, as described above.

Another method is reduction firing of the **raku** type (see page 26). The pot is fired at a temperature required by the glaze composition and when it drops to about 800 °C, the pot is taken out from the kiln and placed in a tub filled with sawdust, wood shavings, hay, shredded paper, etc. The vessel is then tightly closed to make the effect of the smoke, produced by burning organic matter, last as long as possible. In the end the pot is not quenched in water as customary in raku, but is left to cool in the reduction vessel. If removed prematurely, the pot lustre could reoxidize. This applies also to reduction performed in a kiln.

Note that lustre glazes are not identical to lustre paints which yield similar results but use a different technique (see page 90).

SALT GLAZES

Salt glazes are particularly suited for stoneware. During the last stage of the firing, when the body has already completely vitrified on the surface, rock (kitchen) salt is thrown inside the kiln. In an atmosphere saturated with water vapour the salt decomposes into sodium oxide and hydrochloric acid. Sodium oxide reacts with the surface of the hot pot, forming a glaze at about 1190-1290 °C. For 1 cubic metre of kiln space about 2.5 kilogrammes of salt are needed. Adding borax, soda or potash to the salt will produce salt glazes at lower temperatures.

Unlike other glazes, salt glazes are very thin. However, since the glaze is fused with the body, forming a homogeneous substance, rather than deposited on the surface, no crazing occurs. The quality of the glaze depends on the composition of the body. Of great importance is the silica-to-alumina ratio, which should be 3.5:1 to 12:1. Since these glazes are fired at lower temperatures, good glazing requires more silica in the body. Good salt glazing depends also on the fuel used and on the environment in the kiln. Glazes from coal-fired kilns tend to be dark and of a reddish brown coloration, while wares fired in oil or gas-fired kilns are lighter in shade. The most attractive tones are achieved in wood-fired kilns, since the appearance of the glaze is affected by potassium compounds contained in the firewood.

The colour greatly depends on the ferric oxide content and method of firing. Yellow wares will be obtained if salt is thrown in the kiln with an

36
Pots
Rearen (1584) and Siegburg (3rd quarter of 16th
century), Germany
Salt-glazed stoneware, brown and pale grey, with rich
relief decoration
Height 34.5 cm
Private collection

oxidizing atmosphere after firing. When the salt is
dispersed, the kiln is left to cool slowly. If salt is
added in a reducing atmosphere and the kiln is
cooled rapidly, a grey colour will result.

When a red-brown colour is desired, the procedure is the same as with grey wares, but after the
salt is thrown in, the temperature is raised again
(if need be as high as 1290 °C) and only then the
kiln is left to cool down slowly. Rapid cooling
would invariably produce a grey colour.

Some pigment oxides mixed with the salt also
yield interesting colour shades, especially if used
on a white body. For example, manganese carbonate stains purple-red to purple, copper carbonate
blue-green to red, while iron disulphate produces
greenish tones.

Salt glazes probably originated in 12th-century

Some glaze recipes

Rhineland. They are still used there for the traditional manufacture of wine and beer tankards.

Typical of this German stoneware are reliefs painted with coloured enamel on the dried body. They are prepared from 70 per cent pigment oxides and 30 per cent plastic stoneware clay. Copper is unsuitable as a stain since it is absorbed by salt glaze.

One of the disadvantages of salt glazes is that they require a separate kiln since once salt has been used in the kiln, the latter cannot be utilized for firing other wares. Another disadvantage is that salt glaze firing produces hydrogen chloride which inevitably escapes through the flue and pollutes the environment.

An interesting method of salt glaze firing in a normal kiln, known as smearing, was used in 19th-century England, as described by G. Weiss. The pot is placed inside a refractory saggar smeared inside with a thick coat made of 67 parts salt, 28 parts potash and 5 parts litharge. As the ware is fired to 1300 °C, vapours of lead chloride thus produced glaze the body with a thin coat. The saggar lid must be well sealed with kaolin paste to prevent the lead chloride vapours from contaminating the kiln.

Kenzan raku glaze (after Leach)

White lead	50		
Quartz	39	Frit	18
Calcined borax	11	White lead	61
		Unpurified sand from	
		Boshy Island	21

Glaze used by Ogata Kenzan. Fired at 750 °C.

Raku glaze (after Leach)

White lead	66	(Quartz may be
Quartz	30	replaced by river
Kaolin	4	sand.)

Raku glaze used by B. Leach as a substitute for Japanese raku glaze. Fired at 750 °C.

Japanese transparent raku glaze (after Sanders)

Lead frit	10	Lead frit (Shiratama):	
White lead	100	Lead carbonate	39
Quartz	35	Borax	11
		Quartz	39

Glaze used by Kenkichi Tomimoto to overglaze pigments and colours. Fired at 850 °C.

Coloured raku glazes can be prepared by adding pigment oxides. Raku glazes are applied in thick coats, with glue added to prevent peeling.

Black raku glaze (after Lynnggard)

Red lead	50	When taken out of the
Quartz	38	kiln, the pot must be
Kaolin	12	quickly quenched in
Ferric oxide	9	water. Slow cooling
Chromic oxide	3.5	produces a greyish
		brown colour. Fired at
		1150-1200 °C.

Egyptian paste (after Kenny)

Feldspar	34	Self-glazing mix for
Quartz	34	modelling small
Clay	11	figures and jewellery.
Ground soda	5	Must be fired
Sodium bicarbonate	5	suspended on
Dextrin	8	resistance wire.
		Mix 100 g dry mix
		with 2 tablespoons wa-
		ter. Add water drop by
		drop until the mix is
		mouldable. Fired at
		960 °C.

To colour Egyptian paste, add the following to the mix:

Copper carbonate	3	Turkish blue

Cobalt carbonate	1	Blue
Chromic oxide	1	Green
Manganese dioxide	2	Violet
Lead chromate	5	Yellow

Basic alkaline glaze

Feldspar	20	Especially suitable for white body. For use on red or yellow body, add 10 % tin oxide. Fired at 1060 °C.
Chalk	9	
Kaolin	3	
Quartz	25	
Borax	39	
Zinc oxide	9	

To colour the above glaze, add the following:

Cupric oxide	5	Egyptian blue
Cupric oxide	10	Persian blue
Cobalt oxide	0.5	

Turkish blue (after Kenny)

White lead	26	Fired at 1060 °C.
Barium carbonate	10	
Zinc oxide	4	
Colemanite	82	
Feldspar	60	
Kaolin	10	
Quartz	77	
Cupric oxide	10	
Tin oxide	20	

Brown lustre glaze (after Kenny)

White lead	175	Glaze produces attractive lustre effects when fired. Fired at 1060 °C.
Feldspar	39	
Kaolin	13	
Quartz	48	
Manganese carbonate	17	
Ferric oxide	8	

Crystalline glaze (after Kenny)

White lead	237	Good for trials with pigment oxide. Fired at 1120 °C.
Feldspar	37	
Clay	6	
Quartz	51	
Rutile	23	

Especially beautiful crystals will be produced if the glaze above is coloured with the following pigment oxides:

Cobalt oxide	1	Produces light blue matt surface with yellow and blue streaks.
Cupric oxide	8	Produces green matt surface with lighter and darker streaks.
Ferric oxide	16	Produces brown matt surface with yellow crystals.

Crystalline glaze for porcelain (after Hegemann)

Calcined quartz	250	This is a basic underglaze. When fired, it is overglazed with a crystalline glaze. Must be applied in a thick coat. Fired at 1280 °C. Reducing atmosphere.
Feldspar	625	
Limestone	275	
Finely ground potshard (grog)	500	
Calcined clay	100	

The basic glaze above is used to thickly glaze a body of the following composition:

Calcined quartz	35
Feldspar	30
Sedlec kaolin	35
Žatec clay	5

Pots coated with the fired basic glaze given above are then overglazed with a glaze of the following composition:

Zinc oxide	90	To be fired in an oxidizing atmosphere at 1300 °C. Should not cool slowly.
Red lead	10	
Dextrin	8	

Calcareous glaze No. 8 (after Leach)

Kaolin	10	Standard glaze, slightly milky. Good base for colouring with pigment oxides. Fired at 1250-1300 °C.
Limestone	20	
Quartz	30	
Feldspar	40	

Calcareous glaze (after Behrens)

Kaolin	10	Matt glaze for stoneware. Fired at 1250 °C.
Chalk	20	
Quartz	30	
Nepheline syenite	40	

Kawai blue—Ruli (after Leach)

Glaze No. 8	80	Requires reducing conditions. To change tone, add iron, clay, manganese. Fired at 1250-1280 °C.
Feldspar	20	
Cobalt nitrate	0.2	

White matt glaze

Feldspar	28	Porcelain glaze for reducing as well as oxidizing conditions. Fired at 1260-1280 °C.
Quartz	28	
Chalk	12	
Magnesite	17	
Kaolin	15	

Vegetable ash glaze

Mixed ash	50	Basic reduction glaze
Kaolin	50	for work with pigment
		oxides. Fired at
		1260-1280 °C.

Light green celadon (after Leach)

Feldspar	25	Porcelain bodies may
Fern ash	12	be glazed with raw
Limestone	15	glaze. To be fired in
Kaolin	7	a reducing
Clay	20	atmosphere.
Quartz	20	This glaze for soft
Ferric oxide	1	porcelain is to be fired
		at 1250 °C.

Kenzan celadon (after Leach)

Feldspar	62	To be fired in
Vegetable ash	18	a reducing
Kaolin	12	atmosphere.
Quartz	2	Stoneware glaze for
Burnt ochre	6	1230-1280 °C.
Ferric oxide	0.12	

Celadon glaze (after Kuch)

Sodium feldspar	830	Reduction glaze for
Chalk	90	white porcelain or
Quartz	100	stoneware bodies. Add
Ferric oxide	20	glue as required.
		Fired at 1320 °C.

Celadon glaze (after Kenny)

Quartz	134	To be fired in
Floated whiting	80	a reducing
Kaolin	80	atmosphere.
Feldspar	111	Fired at 1250-1320 °C.
Ferric oxide	4	

Red copper glaze (after Leach)

Feldspar	55	Underglaze colour to
Limestone	22	be overglazed with
Lead oxide	4	stoneware glaze No. 8.
Quartz	14	Turns red in an
Tin oxide	3	oxidizing atmosphere,
Cupric oxide	2	green if reduction
		fired. Fired at
		1250-1300 °C.

Red copper glaze (sang de boeuf, after Kenny)

Feldspar	40	Porcelain glaze,
Quartz	40	requires reduction
Powdered borax	12	firing. Fired at
Floated whiting	18	1320 °C.
Copper carbonate	0.5	
Tin oxide	2	
Bentonite	1	

COLOURS, ENGOBES AND PRECIOUS METALS

Pigments

Ceramic colours are based on pigment oxides which have been discussed in the chapter on glazes. Generally speaking, ceramic colours can be divided into **pigments** (used to stain bodies and glazes, enamels, etc.), **high-melting colours** (that is, raw glaze colours, underglaze colours and salts) and **low-melting colours** (on-glaze colours and enamels and lustres).

On-glaze colours which are fired at low temperatures (that is, at about 700 °C) produce an almost inexhaustible range of shades and tones. However, as the temperature of firing rises, the range becomes limited, ending with a few underglaze colours for porcelain. The greatest difficulties are experienced with red, while chrome green and cobalt blues are most stable and withstand even the highest firing temperatures.

Pigment oxides are powerful softeners (that is, they reduce the melting point). The major exception is chromium. Therefore, if pigment oxides are to be used to stain a colourless glaze, it is usually necessary to adjust the formula by changing the flux content. The adjustment must be done separately and specifically for each colour since every oxide has a different effect. This is why pigment oxides are first fused with fire-resistant materials like silica or kaolin to balance their meltability and increase their stability during firing.

The materials are first mixed wet and then thoroughly ground. Excess water is poured off and the mixture is left to dry. Then it is reground to powder and fired in an oxidizing atmosphere at a temperature which should be at least as high as that of glost-firing. The melt is then ground, placed in a deep container and topped with water. After the stain has settled, the water is drawn off and replaced with fresh water. This washing process is repeated six or seven times, then the pigment is dried and ground again to powder.

Pigments and stains are used as a base for colours in or under the glaze, but also for staining engobes.

37
Meiping vase
Seto, Japan, 20th century
Stoneware with engraved decoration under olive green
14th-century *Ko-Seto* glaze
Height 48 cm
National Gallery, Prague

Underglaze paints

Underglaze paints come either in solid or liquid form (powdered or as salt solutions) and are formulated for use within the firing range of 900-1400 °C.

Solid powdered paints are made from pigment oxides or stains by adding 20-50 per cent glaze. Glaze may be replaced partially or totally by feldspar. The paint must have the same porosity as the body to allow the glaze to form a uniform layer over the painted and unpainted places. The content of flux must not be too high, otherwise the decoration may run or become blurred.

The composition and range of colour depend not only on the firing temperature but also on the chemical composition of the body and the glaze. The richest range of underglaze colours is obtained within the temperature range of 900-1100 °C, using white calcareous bodies combined with fritted glazes poor in boric acid. Too much alkali or boric acid in the glaze would weaken and even bleach the colour, especially pink, reddish brown and yellow. Under the same conditions uranium red will turn yellow.

Strong alkaline glazes will turn copper green into turquoise and manganese brown into magenta.

Too much lead, especially unfritted, will combine with chrome colours, producing lead chromate which will stain the glaze yellow. Likewise, a reducing atmosphere will strongly affect some colours: Naples yellow is bleached while titanium yellow turns blue. Chrome colours change to greenish brown, iron-bearing pigments to greyish green (celadon) and copper colours to red (*sang de boeuf*).

If the decoration under the glaze tends to run even though the glaze itself behaves correctly, it is an indication that the paint contains too much flux. This means that the pigment should have

38
Kuan box
China, Yüan dynasty,
13th-14th century
Stoneware,
Lung-ch'üan celadon glaze
Height 22 cm
National Gallery, Prague

more refractory oxides. Prepared paints can be adjusted by adding kaolin.

On the other hand, should the paint contain too little flux, the glaze will blister or dull spots will appear. The cause may also be in a low-melting base pigment, or the paint coat may be too thick, even though the paint may be mixed correctly. water, sometimes turpentine or balsam (see the chapter on decoration, page 141 ff.).

Salt solutions

Solutions of metallic salts are also used for underglaze decoration. Typical examples include nitrates, acetates and chlorides, which are heated and dissolved in glycerine or in a 1:1 mixture of glycerine and water. Sulphates may also be used for this purpose but owing to their lower solubility, weaker solutions will be obtained. The heating should take place in a sand bath and maximum care should be taken since nitrates mixed with glycerine explode at high temperatures. Salts insoluble in glycerine must be dissolved in water, which is then evaporated and the solution diluted with glycerine.

Salt solutions are used on biscuit, exceptionally also on leather-hard, unfired bodies. Prior to glazing, the body decorated with salts must be biscuit-fired to convert soluble chlorides, nitrates, etc. into insoluble oxides and to ensure even absorption of water from the glaze. If the decoration is not biscuit-fired, the colours of the finished glazed pot are much weaker and often penetrate through the body wall to the opposite surface. Some solutions leave such a weak trace on biscuit that it is difficult to tell which places have already been decorated. Such solutions may be stained with aniline dyes which burn out completely in the fire. However, no gold-bearing salts should be stained, since organic substances contained in the stain would spoil the solution.

Large surfaces or bodies can be sprayed to advantage, because the coloration is uniform. Dark patches in the decoration indicate that the salt solution is too thick and must be diluted.

The following salts may be used as colorants (after Berdel):

Blue	cobalt chloride, cobalt nitrate
Green	chromium chloride, chromium nitrate
Brown	manganese chloride (other shades can be obtained if iron or chromium is added), nickel nitrate, iron chloride with 0.25 or 0.5 chromium chloride
Yellow-brow	iron chloride
Yellow	uranyl nitrate
Dark brown to black	a mixture of cobalt, nickel, iron and chromium salts
Pink	gold chloride
Grey	a mixture of cobalt and nickel salts, or platinum chloride

A whole range of tones can be obtained by mixing individual solutions, but the colour will also be affected by the composition of the body and the glaze as well as by the firing temperature and the atmosphere in the kiln. For example, chromium salts turn brown due to iron contained in the body, while barium or sodium in the glaze will also affect the colour, as will a reducing atmosphere.

Since salt solutions give the body soft pastel shades, it is imperative that the overglaze should be as transparent as possible.

39
Tulip vase
Adriaen Kocks, 'De Grieksche A' workshop, Delft,
Holland, 1687-1701
Faience with blue decoration
Height 29 cm
Museum of Decorative Arts, Prague

40
Plate
Casa Pirota, Faenza, Italy, 1540
Maiolica, pale blue glaze painted with *bianco sopra
azzuro*; orange figure
Diameter 24.5 cm
Museum of Decorative Arts, Prague

Paints used in raw glaze (enamel)

These paints are used for decoration applied on raw powder glazes. They are made from the same pigments as underglaze paints but must be much softer to fuse well with the glaze and produce the required gloss when glost-fired. The painting is usually done on a white opaque tin glaze. The application is as in the case of underglaze paints but the coat applied must be thicker. The paints are mixed with water, sometimes with a few drops of glycerine added. Another method is painting between two layers of glaze. Higher-melting colours are used and the finished decoration is sprayed with a thin coat of low-melting transparent glaze which produces high gloss when fired. The method originated in Italy where local potters used a low-melting glaze known as *coperta* for their faience wares. Both techniques discussed above are used almost exclusively for maiolica (that is, at about 1000 °C).

Painting into raw glaze is a technique which has been widely used in the history of pottery. The best examples include Islamic, Italian, Delft and Habaner faience and maiolica wares. Literature sometimes terms these paints used in raw glazes as 'high fire colours'.

On-glaze colours

Paints used on fired glaze, sometimes also known as muffle or low fire colours, are low-melting lead or boron glazes stained with pigments or metallic oxides. The on-glaze in this case acts as a flux and heat fuses the colour with the glaze. Pigments are usually mixed with flux in the proportion of 1 part pigment to 2-4 parts flux to produce glossy colours or 1 part pigment to 1 part flux for matt colours. The proportion is adjusted according to the firing temperature and melting point of the flux. Different colours require different fluxes; for example, blacks need more lead, while browns require less lead, and reds will be brighter if they have more lime.

Prepared colours are tested in coats of various thickness applied to the fired body. The coats should have the same gloss after firing and the difference in thickness should only produce different tones. If the colour turns out cloudy, that is too opaque, more flux should be added or the firing temperature increased. Opacity is also caused by water vapour or by reduction. If crazing occurs, the flux should be changed or the firing temperature adjusted.

These paints are thinned with essential (volatile) oils, but also sugar, honey, syrup, etc. Essential oils are aromatic substances which will evaporate at a given temperature, leaving resinous, strongly adhesive substances like copal balsam, thick turpentine oil, lavender or clove oil, etc.

The colours are ground using a spatula or glass muller which also serves as a palette. Sufficient thinner is added to ensure that the paint does not become blotchy but adheres to the surface even when applied in thick coats (enamel) and large areas. If slower drying is required, a few drops of clove oil should be added to the mixed paint.

Small quantities of prepared paint can be stored for future use, if kept in closed porcelain jars. After use, the paint in the jar should be covered with a thin layer of turpentine or some other oil. Prior to use, the oil is poured off, not mixed with the paint.

On-glaze colours are used for painting, spraying and printing. They are fired exclusively in an oxidizing atmosphere at 600-800 °C. Formerly, each colour had to be fired separately, so that the pot had to be refired as much as six or seven times, each time at a slightly lower temperature, but today commercial colours are formulated for the same temperature so that the pot is fired only once, possibly twice if gold is also used.

Slips (engobes)

HIGH RELIEF ENAMELS

These are opaque colours which are applied very thickly on the body. They have a high melting point and therefore retain their relief on firing. They are used to create raised ornamentation and are mixed in the same way, using the same thinners, as on-glaze colours.

ON-GLAZE HIGH FIRE COLOURS

Fired glazes are sometimes decorated by painting or printing and refired in high temperatures. For this purpose underglaze colours can be used, but they must be softened with glaze or some other flux. They are ground and applied in the same way as on-glaze colours. When fired at a high temperature, the colours penetrate the glaze, producing a decoration very much like that of underglaze colours, but in this case with slightly blurred outlines.

LUSTRE COLOURS

Lustre colours will produce similar effects to lustre glazes, but the process does not involve reduction. Chemically, these paints are resinates, or resinous metal soaps, that is, melts of rosin (colophony) and some pigment metal nitrate. The melt dissolved in lavender or rosemary oil is applied to the fired glaze with a brush or sprayed in thin coats and then fired at about 700°C, which results in a thin iridescent metal coat. Depending on the metal salt used, it is either colourless (bismuth, lead, zinc) or coloured: blue (cobalt), green (chromium), pink (gold with bismuth), etc.

PRECIOUS METALS

Solutions of precious metals are made in a similar way to lustre colours. The metals used in this fashion include burnished silver, dull and burnished gold and platinum.

Metals are applied with a brush and fired at about 750°C. Gold and platinum are shiny immediately, while silver and dull gold must be burnished after firing with a piece of agate mounted on a handle. Either the entire surface is burnished or a design can be brought up on the dull background.

Engobes, known also as slips, are composed of natural or artificially coloured clays and are used for coating bodies of different composition or colour. They are also used to coat bodies made from coarse-grained or impure clays and constitute a basic material for various slip decoration techniques.

The composition must be adjusted to the shrinkage of the body, that is the slip must have a lower shrinkage than the body since the latter is solid while the slip is liquid.

Basic white slips are composed of a mixture of white plastic and non-plastic clays, kaolin, floated whiting and other materials. The base for porcelain slip is porcelain paste.

Coloured slips are obtained by staining white base slips with oxides or stains. The quantity of the colorant to be used is determined by the required depth of colour. Slips are applied by pouring, dipping, spraying and other techniques discussed in greater detail in the chapter dealing with decoration.

41
In a Gallery
Jindra Viková, Czechoslovakia, 1985
Electroporcelain with relief lugs, combined underglaze and on-glaze painting; electrically fired at 1300 °C
Height 80 cm
Private collection

Some pigment recipes

Kenzan raku pigments (after Leach)

Black

China cobalt	67	China cobalt may be replaced by:	
White lead	7		
Frit	26	Manganese trioxide	40
		Ferrous oxide	30
		Cobalt oxide	20
		Burnt ochre	10

White

Kaolin	40
White lead	40
Frit	10
Quartz	10

Green

Copper carbonate	19
White lead	26
Frit	48
Quartz	7

Yellow

Antimony trioxide	$2\frac{1}{3}$
White lead	$32\frac{2}{3}$
Frit	64
Ferric oxide	1

Red

Burnt ochre	62	When fired at 700°, the ochre should be reddish or light red.
Ferric oxide	8	
White lead	15	
Frit	15	

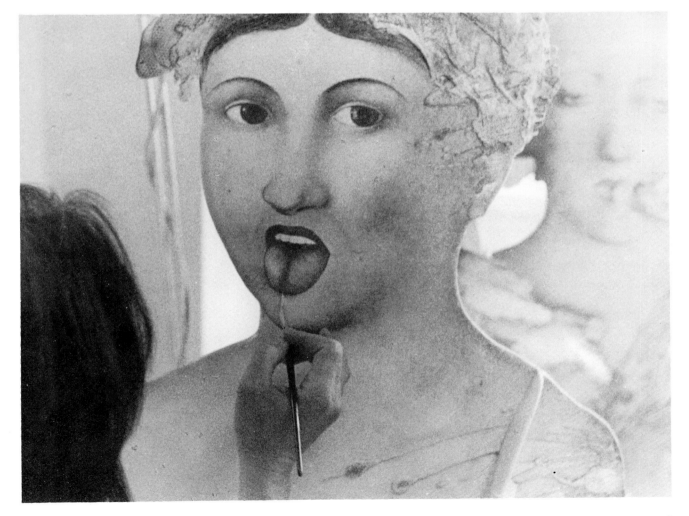

Brown

Black pigment	50
Red pigment	50

Blue

Enamel	25	This enamel used by the Japanese painter and potter Ogata Kenzan (1660-1743) can be substituted with blue enamel with 10% ground glass cullet and 1-5% ferric oxide.
White lead	37.5	
Frit	37.5	

Japanese Shiratama frit

White lead	50
Quartz	39
Calcined borax	11

Black pigment used under green

Manganese dioxide	70
Cobalt monoxide	10
Quartz	20

Kawai's red copper pigment

Cupric oxide	60	Rice straw ash may be substituted with wheat straw or bran ash. Carbon particles contained in the ash facilitate local reduction.
Zinc oxide	28	
Tin dioxide	3	
Hard rice straw ash	9	
Barium monoxide	10	

Lustre colours (after Passeri)

Copper sulphate	10	*Gold lustre (Persian)*
Ferrous sulphate	5	
Silver sulphate	1	
Ochre	12	

Copper sulphate	5	*Gold metallic lustre*
Silver sulphate	2	
Colcothar	1	
Bole	4	

Silver oxide	8	*Red metallic lustre*
Ferrous oxide	5	
Colcothar	6	
Bole	6	

Cuprous sulphate	10	*Dark gold (Syrian) lustre*
Ferrous sulphate	5	
Silver sulphate	1	
Black oxide of manganese	12	

Cuprous sulphate	5	*Red (Baghdad) lustre*
Tin oxide	2	
Soot	1	
Ochre	4	

Cuprous sulphate	10	*Pale gold (Moorish) lustre*
Ferrous sulphate	5	
Silver sulphate	1	
Chalk	12	

Lustre colours are ground with vinegar and thick oil of turpentine (for thinning with turpentine) or with vinegar and gum arabic (for thinning with water). They are applied to fired maiolica glazes and reduction fired at 650-700 °C.

Underglaze salt solutions

Note: Bé units used below signify density in Baumé degrees.

Carmine

Gold trichloride	10 g
Aluminium chloride 15 Bé solution to make	100 ml

Violet

Gold chloride	10 g
Cobalt dichloride	32 g
Aluminium chloride 15 Bé solution to make	100 ml

Turquoise

Cobalt dichloride	36 g
Dextrin	4.5 g
Chromium trichloride (50% solution)	50 ml
Aluminium chloride 15 Bé solution to make	100 ml

Pea green
Cobalt dichloride	2.5 g
Chromium trichloride (50% solution)	90 ml
10% solution of boric acid in glycerine	9 ml

Ochre
Manganese dichloride	60 g
Distilled water to make	100 ml

Brown
Nickel dichloride	38 g
Distilled water to make	100 ml
Dextrin	9 g

Blue
Cobalt dichloride	100 g
Zinc dichloride	5 g
Glycerine	24 ml
Dextrin	6.4 g
Distilled water to make	144 ml

Grey
Iron trichloride	28 g
Cobalt dichloride	6.4 g
Chromium trichloride (50% solution)	9 ml
Glycerine solution (15 Bé) to make	100 ml

Bleaching salt
Zinc dichloride (1:1 solution)	50 ml
Aluminium chloride (20 Bé solution)	50 ml
Dextrin	9 g

An application of this salt onto a colouring salt solution facilitates a deeper penetration of the latter into the body, making the tone paler. Applicable only to pale tone solutions.

Examples of some salt mixtures

Yellow-brown
Pea-green salt	40	Thinner 1a or 1b
Ochre salt	60	(see below)

Purple
Carmine salt	80	Thinner 3
Violet salt	20	

Blue-green
Turquoise salt	10	
Pea-green salt	20	Thinner 2
Thinner	60	

Coffee
Carmine salt	80	Thinner 3
Turquoise salt	20	

Olive green
Pea-green salt	10	Thinner 1a or 1b
Brown salt	10	

Flesh
Brown salt	10	Thinner 1a or 1b
Thinner	60	

Salt solution thinners
Aluminium chloride (15 Bé solution)	50 ml	Thinner 1a
Glycerine (15 Bé solution)	50 ml	
Aluminium chloride (15 Bé solution)	50 ml	Thinner 1b
Sugar (15 Bé solution)	50 ml	
Solution of glycerine and distilled water (density of solution 15 Bé)		Thinner 2
Solution of aluminium chloride and distilled water (density of solution 15 Bé)		Thinner 3

BEWARE: Dissolving of chloride in water should be performed under a fume hood or in a fume cupboard, or in open air. Breathing of the gas which is given off is dangerous!

MODELLING AND MOULDING

Tools and workshop equipment

Fig. 25   Plastering tools:
(a-c) Steel tools of various shapes for retouching
(d-e) Loop tools
(f) Multi-purpose knife
(g, h) Files for working rounded surfaces
(for example, when making handles)
(i, j) Wooden mallet and chisel for splitting moulds
(k) Draw knife for shaping outer surgaces of moulds
(l) Mason's ladle for mixing plaster
(m) Spoon for mixing and handling plaster
(n) Scraper for working flat surfaces
(o) Calipers

Modelling and moulding are so much associated with plaster-of-Paris that the chapter could be well termed 'plaster-work'. Plaster-work should be done preferably in a separate room or at least in a place far from where clays and glazes are handled, since even a small piece of plaster can cause great trouble in firing.

The most important piece of equipment is a potter's wheel for turning plaster models. The wheel can be of the traditional foot-operated type or it can be driven by an electric motor (fig. 28). Another indispensable piece of equipment is a sturdy working table topped with a marble slab. Wooden top tables must be clad with zinc-plated sheet steel, but a thick glass plate embedded in plaster is also serviceable.

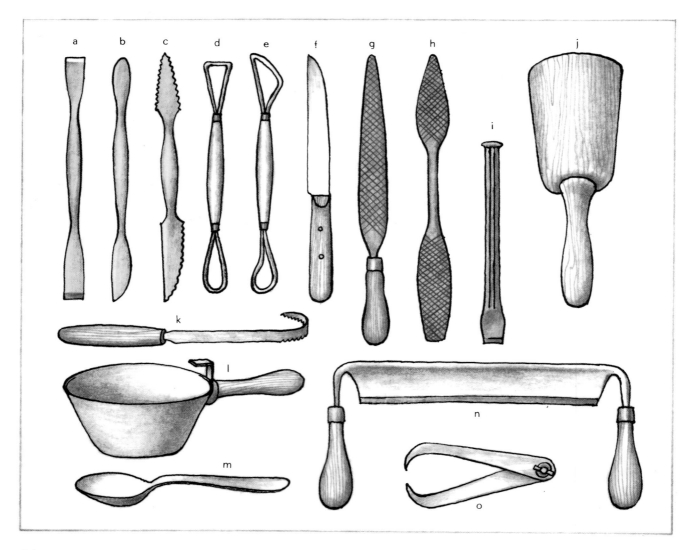

XVI
Tankard
Kreussen, Germany, 1665
Stoneware with salt glaze and coloured enamels,
pewter trimmings
Height 15.5 cm
Museum of Decorative Arts, Prague

XVII
Hexagonal flask
Slovakia, about 1700
Habaner faience with tin screwcap
Height 30 cm
Museum of Decorative Arts, Prague

XVIII
Pot with lid
West Moravia, Czechoslovakia, 1798
Faience, buff body
Height 33 cm
Ethnographical Museum, Prague

XIX
Clock
Sèvres, France, 1875
Porcelain decorated with on-glaze
painting and gold
Height 45 cm
Museum of Decorative Arts, Prague

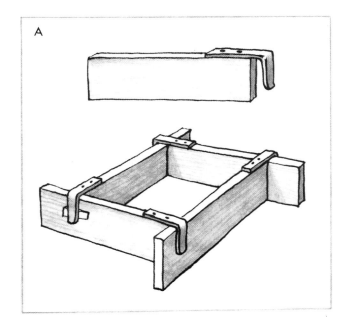

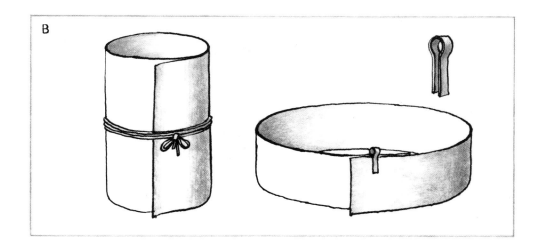

Fig. 26
(A)   Wooden planks
(B)   Sheet metal for
mould making

strips but stiff oiled paper will do as well. Irregular shapes are best outlined by strips of lead sheet. To border smaller areas, modelling clay is normally used. The same material is used to stop gaps in moulds bordered with other materials.

There is also a whole number of substances needed for the preparation and separation of the mould and the model.

Shellac dissolved in alcohol: thick shellac is used for glueing, while thin shellac is used to treat models prior to casting.

Varnish: in ceramic factories dry models are treated with hot varnish instead of shellac.

Soft soap: 1 part grain soap is boiled with 3 parts water and whisked to foam using a brush. When cool, it is whisked again with 5-10 per cent oil. It is used to soap models prior to casting.

Water soap: 40 per cent soft soap boiled with 60 per cent water.

Plaster mixing requires a number of vessels of different sizes, water buckets, ladles and scoops used by plasterers and special rubber bowls made specifically for mixing plaster. Most of the tools used for plaster work are illustrated in fig. 25; others will be discussed in this chapter.

Apart from the items listed above, a standard set of workshop tools is required: that is, hammer, pliers, vice, drill, files, metal cutters, wood saw and hacksaw, nails, screws, wire, sheet steel, brushes, natural sponge and other items.

Strips of wood come in handy, because they can be used to form moulds (see fig. 26). Round shapes can be made from zinc or aluminium sheet

Wood oil: used to coat models and moulds prior to soaping. Immediately before the plaster is cast, the soap foam and oil are wiped off with a wet sponge.

Stearin or **paraffin** dissolved in kerosene: used to coat the bottom plate of mould, the borders and all parts that must be isolated.

Models are slicked with thin steel sheets (0.1-0.3 mm thick), fine abrasive and emery papers, while the final smoothing, producing a glassy surface, is done with horsetail (*equisetum*) stalks which have been steeped in water.

A vital piece of equipment has been designed to prevent plaster clogging the drain. It is shown in

Fig. 27 Schematic diagram of a sink with a dirt trap

fig. 27. Plaster contained in the water is trapped in a dirt trap and settles at the bottom, so that only clean water leaves the trap. Sedimented dirt is periodically removed.

PLASTER-OF-PARIS

Plaster is not only used for making models and moulds but has a much wider use in ceramics and, therefore, deserves to be discussed in detail.

Plaster is produced by heating and grinding gypsum. The firing temperature determines its hardness and setting time. For example, plaster fired at about 1000 °C sets after about 24 hours or even longer and is very hard. For ceramic use the so-called alabaster or modelling plaster is best. It is fired at temperatures up to 200 °C and sets in about 15 minutes.

Plaster is always mixed by adding it to water, never the other way round. The water used should be at room temperature and both the water and the plaster should be precisely weighed. (Figures given below refer to parts by weight.)

For hard moulds	64	plaster to	36 water
For standard moulds	58		42
For soft moulds	50		50
For very soft moulds	46		54

However, in common studio practice the ingredients are not weighed but plaster is simply added to water until it ceases to absorb the latter and a small amount of the plaster is seen above the surface. After a few minutes the top disintegrates. While adding the plaster to water, the former should be rubbed to break any hard lumps which would be difficult to mix smoothly. When all plaster disappears under the surface, the mixture must be thoroughly stirred (preferably by hand) to a smooth consistency without any clots. Mixing should be slow and care should be taken not to form air bubbles. Once mixed, no more plaster or water should be added to the mix, nor should a set mix be stirred again.

If rapid setting is required, plaster is mixed with warm water (about 40 °C) or a small amount of salt is added. Setting is slowed by adding milk, vinegar, alum or glue. The latter two materials are also added to increase the strength of the cast.

To increase mould porosity, silicic acid is added. This, however, renders plaster much softer and it must be hardened again. According to Hegemann, the following solution is prepared to remedy the situation: 15 g sodium sulphate, 15 g magnesium chloride, 10 g magnesium carbonate and 25 g cement are added to 1 litre of a 3 per cent solution of silicic acid. One part of the resulting solution is then mixed with one part plaster. A thin mix thus produced is then stirred until it begins to set, then it is cast and left to harden. Finished casts are dried in air for several days. The strength of such hardened but highly porous moulds is 13 kg/cm^2, compared with 3-6 kg/cm^2 in regular moulds.

Modelling figures

Modelling hollow wares

Generally speaking, ceramic models can be divided into two categories: those for figural ceramics and those for hollow wares. Models of the first group are usually made in the same way and using the same materials as in other branches of sculpture. (Therefore, methods of making constructions, modelling and casting are not discussed here in detail since there exist many specialized publications on the subject in which the reader will find detailed information.) Naturally, any composition of a ceramic figure must, from the very beginning, consider the ceramic material to be used, for example, stoneware, porcelain, etc. However, the designer must consider not only aesthetic but also technological aspects, that is, the behaviour of the material in preparation, drying and firing. Simple figures can be hand-built directly from the working material, that is, without a plaster mould, but more complicated work must be modelled from clay, wax or plasticine using a metal or wire armature and then cast in plaster. A finished plaster model is then used to make a mould.

Models of this category are usually cast in plaster using various methods, the most important of which are discussed below.

MODELLING ON A WHEEL

Round plaster shapes are made on a vertical lathe, in principle a potter's wheel, but of different dimensions and design and featuring a large heavy flywheel to give the wheel sufficient momentum. On the side there are movable supports bearing a bar against which the potter steadies his hand as he turns the model (fig. 36). The bench seat is inclined to allow the potter to brace himself and steady his body. A thick plaster wheelhead may be equipped with a mechanical lock facilitating rapid attachment of auxiliary slabs, spindles, rings, etc. (fig. 29).

The model is attached by means of a steel spindle (fig. 33). It is a tapering bar or mandril of a square or triangular section. At the thicker end it flares into a cross which is embedded in a plaster slab, known as a bat. Spindles of various

42
Bird, ritual pipe
Peru, Chimizo culture, 1200-1450
Smoked, partially slicked buff body
22 × 23 cm
Private collection

Fig. 28   *Plastering wheel*

Fig. 29   *Plastering wheelhead with bat, lock, and spindle*

Fig. 30   *Several profiles of turning tools*

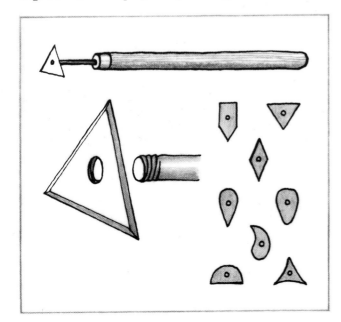

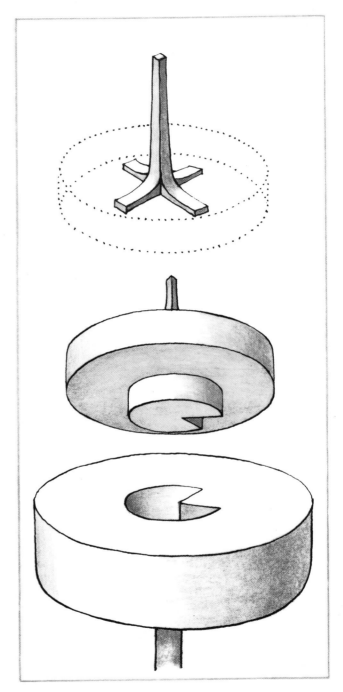

lengths are used: shorter ones for dishes and plates, longer ones for vases and pots.

The rotating model is turned with steel turning tools of various sizes and shapes. Fig. 31 shows several different turning tools which can be fitted into a drill chuck mounted on the end of a wooden handle about 60 cm long. During turning the free end of the tool is held firmly under the arm and the working end is rested against the support bar. The cutting tips are either riveted or attached by means of a screw head (fig. 30) which permits using different tools with a single handle and also greatly facilitates sharpening.

Figs 32-37 Turning plaster models on vertical lathe (plastering wheel or 'whirler')

Figure 32: A plaster bat bearing a spindle is placed over the wheelhead. A lock on the underside fits into a recess cut in the wheelhead.

Fig. 31 A selection of plaster turning tools

Figure 33: The spindle bearing slab is attached to the wheelhead using a coil of soft clay.

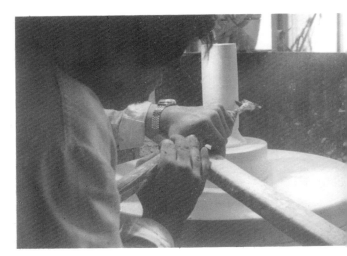

Figure 34: The steel spindle, that is, the axis of the model to be built, is enclosed with sheet metal and a sufficient quantity of plaster is poured in. Duralumin strips are best, but stiff waxed or oiled paper will also do, especially pressboard. The sheet is used to make a cylinder and held in shape with a length of string wound round several times. All places where plaster could leak must be stopped with clay. Both the metal mould and the plaster slab must be thoroughly greased and soaped prior to casting. The metal mould is removed when the poured plaster has set but is still plastic.

Figure 36: Rough-shaping of the model is performed with plaster turning tools. The right hand and arm press the free end of the tool handle against the body, while the left hand guides the cutting tool on the model. To have better stability and a firmer hand, the potter uses the support bar which can be adjusted both vertically and horizontally. The cutting edges must be kept clean during the operation as hardened plaster stuck to the edge would produce grooves on the model surface.

Figure 37: The dimensions of the turned model are checked against the drawing, using calipers. The height and profile of the model are checked by means of a template. In fact, the sweep mould can be used for this purpose.

Figure 35: The plaster cylinder is then rough-shaped using a strickle (sweep mould or template). This must be done rapidly while the plaster is still plastic. The sweep mould can be either cut from sheet metal or from a plaster slab, as shown in the picture. To facilitate cleaning, plaster sweep moulds (templates) are impregnated with shellac.

TURNING PLASTER MODELS ON A CRANK

This method is rather laborious but its main advantage is that it permits turning delicate and complicated shapes, which could only be built on a wheel with difficulty. Since the method involves the use of a template, the model is absolutely identical to the drawing.

The construction consists of two U-bent supports bearing a template. Each support carries a bearing and the two bearings carry a tapering shaft of a square or triangular section and fitted with a crank at the thicker end. The bearings must facilitate easy removal of the shaft during the operation.

The template is cut and filed to shape from sheet metal according to the drawing and then nailed to a board of suitable shape. Thicker plywood is best. The edge of the template must extend about 0.5 cm over that of the board.

Figs 38-41   Making a plaster model on a crank

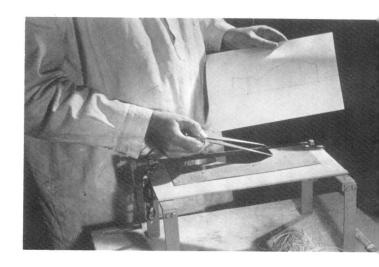

Figure 38: The template board must be positioned exactly according to the drawing (precise measurement is required), because even a minute deviation would result in distorted shape.

Figure 39: The shaft is then wrapped with wood wool, crumpled paper, burlap or similar material and secured with a string. The material must take well to plaster in the early phase of building up the model. Besides, its function is to make the model lighter. Before starting to build up, the wood wool or whatever material is used for the purpose must be wetted, otherwise it would ab-

sorb water from the plaster. During the early stage
it is advisable to use a more solid plaster which
sticks better to the wrapped shaft. The plaster applied onto the rotating shaft is shaped by the template. Note that the shaft must always rotate in
one direction, that is bearing downward onto the
template edge.

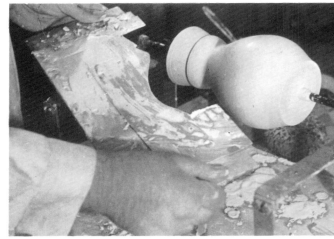

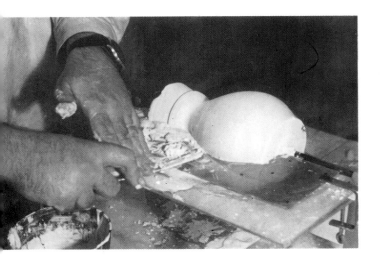

Figure 41: The finished model is easily removed
from the shaft and after plugging the shaft holes
the model can be cast to make a mould.

Figure 40: During rotation plaster is accumulat-
ed on the template. These accumulations must be
continuously removed. This is why it is advisable
to use a design that would permit removing the
shaft together with the built-up model enabling
cleaning of the template. Cleaning is especially
important before giving the model final shape. To
give the model a smooth surface the last plaster
applied should be thin.

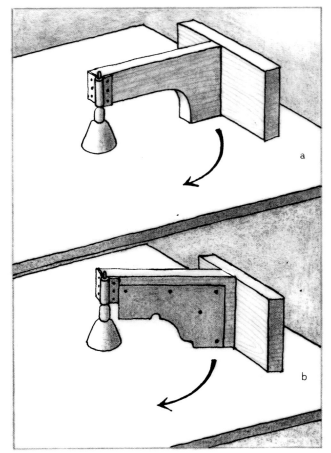

*Fig. 42   Turning plaster models with
a sweep mould:
(a) using a rotating crossbar
(b) sheet metal sweep mould of a dish*

SHAPING BY TEMPLATES

The crank can be used to build up only tall wares, such as vases, pots, etc. Bowls, dishes and other flatwares are shaped on the equipment shown in fig. 42.

The base or bottom of an oblong dish is made by using a template (former) as shown in fig. 43. The profiled template used to give the clay shape is guided by crossboards which help the template to maintain a constant angle with the side bar. All elements must be well smoothed and soaped to facilitate easy travel. Note that the template must always travel in the same direction. The finished profile is then cut and the pieces luted as shown in fig. 44.

The base of an oblong dish with rounded corners is made as follows: the base is shaped in the same way as described above. Using the same template, a circular clay profile is made, which is then cut and luted to the oblong base (fig. 45).

There is also a method which can be used for

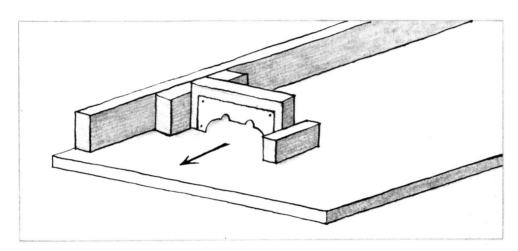

Fig. 43 Making plaster profiles with a template

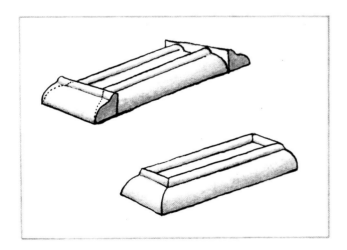

Fig. 44 Modelling an oblong tetragonal dish

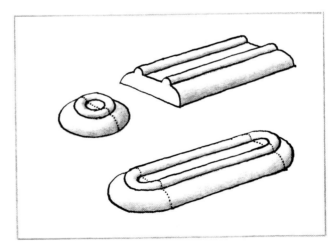

Fig. 45 Making an oblong dish with rounded corners

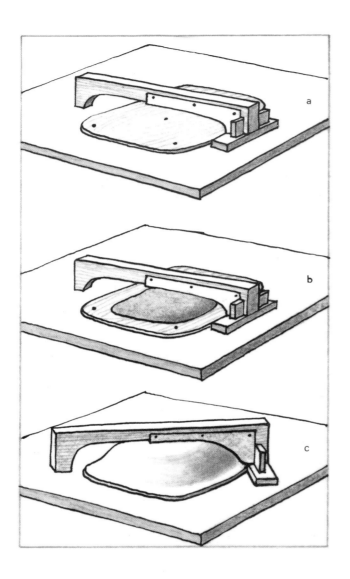

dishes of any shape. The principle remains the same but the guide of the profile is not a plank but a wooden or plaster slab cut to conform to the required shape of the dish (fig. 46).

The last method is similar. The plan of a dish is drawn on a wooden or plaster slab and the dish is then hand built on it from clay or another plastic material. The profile is checked with a template. Clay models can then be cast and finished (fig. 47).

Fig. 46   Making a tetragonal dish:
(a) A plate in the shape of the dish plan is fixed to the plastering table. It is used to guide the template
(b) To make the model lighter and save plaster, the plate can be covered with a heap of clay which is later scooped out of the model
(c) Shaping the dish using a template

Fig. 47   Hand building a model:
(a) The plan of the item is drawn on a plank or plaster slab
(b) The article is built by hand, checking the profile with a template
(c) The finished model is cast in plaster

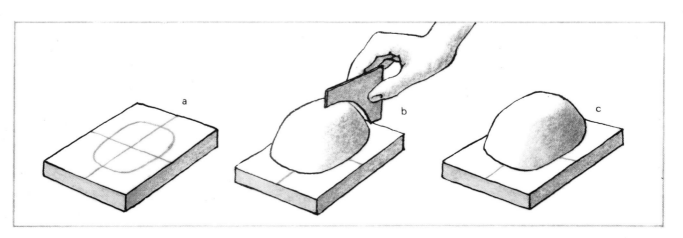

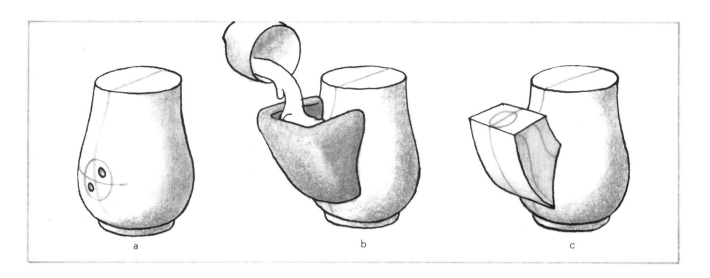

Fig. 48   Modelling a spout:
(a) Quoins are cut in the place where the spout will be jointed to the body of the pot and the whole area is soaped
(b) The future spout is boxed with clay and cast in plaster
(c) The plaster cast is rough shaped and all profiles are drawn; it is possible to take the spout off the body since the quoins facilitate realignment

Fig. 49   Plaster slab with drawn handle profile

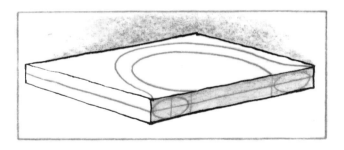

FITTINGS

Handles, lips and spouts are cut from plaster blocks as shown in fig. 49.

A handle profile is drawn on a plaster slab and cut to rough shape with a knife (fig. 49). The edges are smoothed with scrapers and files and the final shape is finished with fine abrasive papers and cast in a mould (fig. 50).

A plaster lug for spout modelling is cast directly on the model. The place where the spout is attached to the teapot is enclosed with clay and cast with plaster. When the plaster begins to harden, it is rough-shaped with a knife and then finished in the same way as a handle (fig. 48).

Mention must be made of the method of making plaster models of pots decorated with modelled reliefs. The relief is cut or modelled for only one quarter of the item (naturally if the item in question can be divided into four equal parts by two planes). The finished quarter is then cast several times and two quarter casts are luted to make one half, and two halves to make the whole item.

Fig. 50   Finished handle mould

Moulds

The main material for mould making is plaster-of-Paris which has almost totally replaced the biscuit clay used in the past.

The making of a split mould of the vase built on a crank and discussed above will become clear from the following illustrations.

The model is divided into two exact halves using a set square or the method shown in fig. 51.

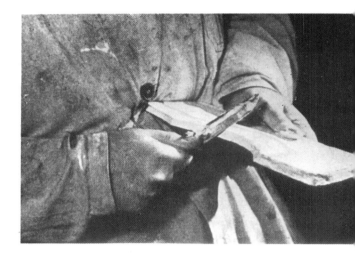

Figure 52: From a plaster slab right-hand and left-hand templates are cut. The two halves are used to make a mould. Templates may also be made from other materials, for example, greased cardboard. Prior to casting the mould the model (core) must be dressed with shellac.

Fig. 51   Dividing a model vertically

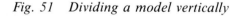

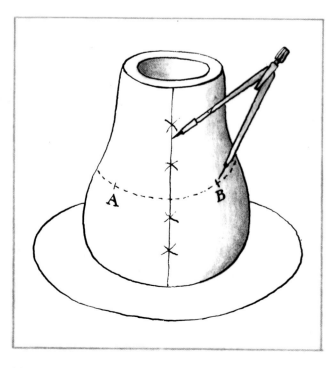

Figure 53: The two templates are placed against the parting plane of the model and enough clay is packed under them to keep them horizontal. The joint between the templates and the model is sealed with clay.

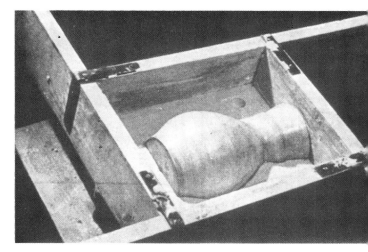

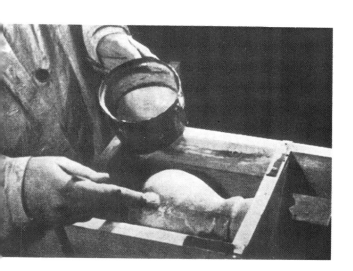

Figure 54: The model is walled with board and all gaps are sealed with clay. Note that all elements must be well soaped. The mould is then cast in plaster.

Figure 56: The model and templates are now used to make the other half-mould. Note that all elements should be resoaped.

Figure 55: The cast half-mould must now be provided with notches so that the two halves tally.

Figure 57: A finished two-part mould. Note that since the vase has no foot ring, the mould need not have a separate base part.

Models can also be simply placed in clay without any plaster template. In this case, a clay block is built up as high as the parting plane of the model, levelled and smoothed with a spatula.

A two-part mould of a different type can be seen in fig. 58. Vases of a tall, tapering shape can be divided horizontally. Moulds of this type have a great advantage in that they can be turned on a wheel without any laborious pattern making.

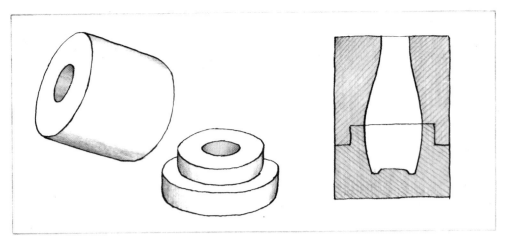

Fig. 58 A two-part hor-izontally split mould

Fig. 59 Vertically split mould with a plug for the bottom

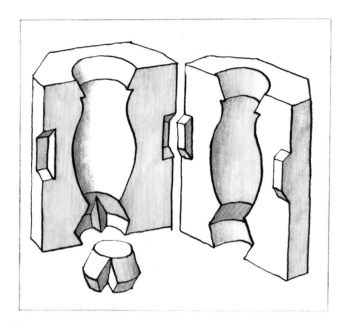

The model and the bottom plug are then coated with a plaster jacket which is turned to the required shape and thickness with turning tools. When the jacket hardens, it is split open with wedges. The procedure is apparent from figs 60, 61.

(a) The mould is partially cut along a marked line using a broad-bladed saw.

(b) Several wooden wedges are placed in the incision. By tapping lightly on the wedges the mould is split to the pattern.

(c) The same procedure is repeated on the other side of the mould and the core is removed.

Split moulds fit well together and leave only a very minute seam on the cast. However, if slip penetrates between the joints, the rough, matching surfaces of the two half-moulds are very difficult to clean.

Fig. 62 shows an interesting method of mould splitting used also in death-mask making. On the model, a pack thread is attached with vaseline along the parting plane of the mould. The model is then cased and cast in plaster. Needless to say, the ends of the thread must be long enough to extend outside. When the plaster has set enough to retain shape but is still soft, the thread is used to cut the mould apart. Since moulds made in this way have no tallying locks, slip must be used to keep the two halves together.

The vase mould shown in fig. 59 is split vertically and features a tapering plug for the bottom. The piece can be made on a wheel at the same time as the model.

Split moulds are very popular and these are turned on the wheel together with the model. First the bottom plug is turned and a notch is cut in it.

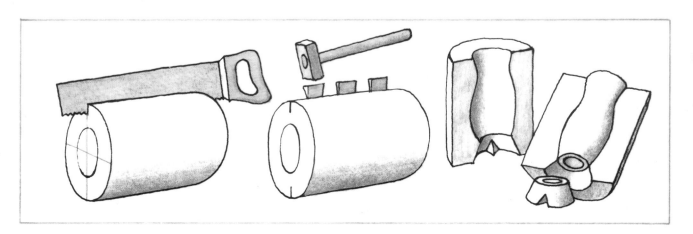

The last type are the so-called piece moulds (fig. 63). They consist of a number of tapering pieces fitting together. The design greatly facilitates assembly and disassembly.

The making of piece moulds for figures composed of dozens of pieces is very complicated and requires long practical experience.

Since piece moulds deteriorate due to repeated casting, plate rims, spouts, handles and small fit-

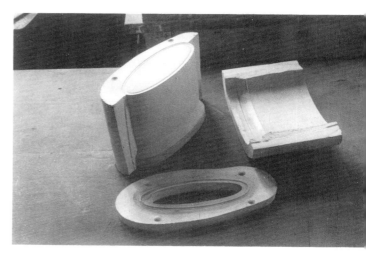

Fig. 61 A split mould with a model of an oval pot

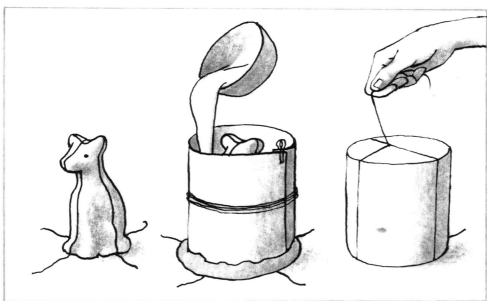

Fig. 62 Parting a mould with a pack thread

Fig. 63 A four-part mould

Fig. 64 Epoxy resin mould

◀ Fig. 60 Making split moulds

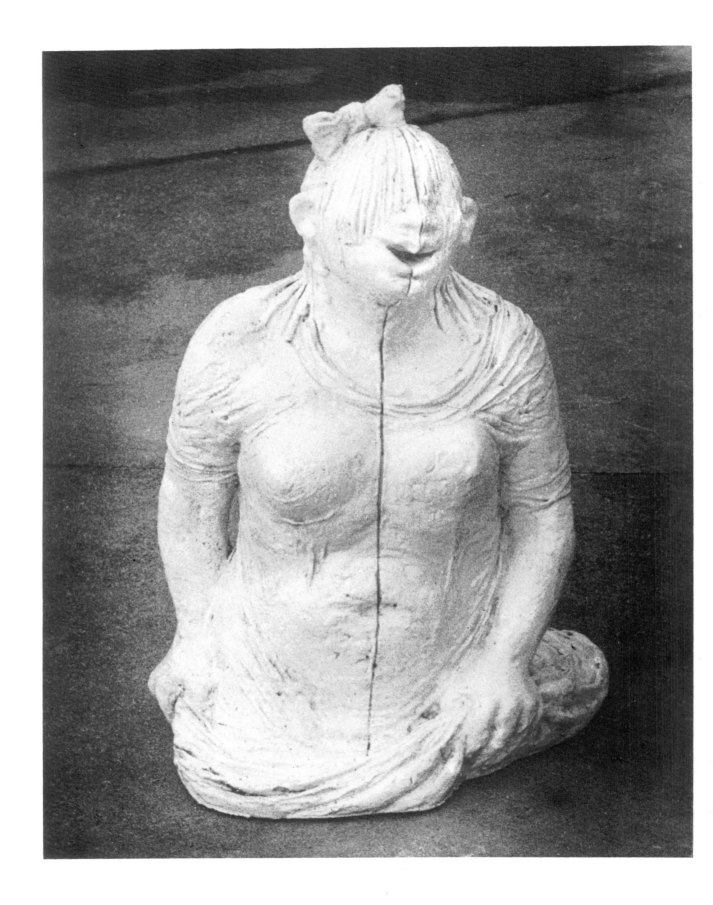

43
Wet Julia
Bohuslav Zemánek, Czechoslovakia, 1974
Porous ware clay with fireclay, glazed with white
opaque glaze; modelled sculpture was used to make
an auxiliary plaster mould which was then
hand-pressed with clay; electrically fired at 1100 °C
80 × 60 cm
Private collection

XX
Pocket watch case
Italy (?), 19th century
Porous ware decorated with painting over fired glaze
Height 26 cm
Private collection

XXI
Egg
Joan Miró, Spain, 1963
Stoneware
180 × 135 cm
Background:
Goddess
1963
Stoneware
157 × 115 cm
Fondation Maeght, Saint-Paul-de-Vence

XXII
Corrida
Pablo Picasso, France, 1949
Porous ware painted with slips and paints under
transparent glaze; electrically fired at
about 1000 °C
32 × 38 cm
Muzeum Narodowe, Warsaw

tings are made from a melt three parts weight rod
sulphur and two parts graphite powder.

Recently, epoxy resins have found a wide use in
mould making. Resins are used to cast master
moulds or to impregnate plaster moulds and models. For impregnation, 40 g epoxy resin and hard-
ener (curing agent) are mixed with 60 g acetone.
Moulds impregnated with this solution need not
be dressed with shellac (fig. 64).

XXIII
Sculpture
Carlo Zauli, Italy, 1978
Stoneware with coloured glaze; electrically fired at
1200 °C
50 × 60 × 22 cm
Private collection

FORMING

Broadly speaking, forming includes all manual or machine procedures used to produce a semi-finished product from ceramic batches.

Fig. 65   Preparing a head model for firing. Using a scoop, all surplus clay is scooped out (see arrows)

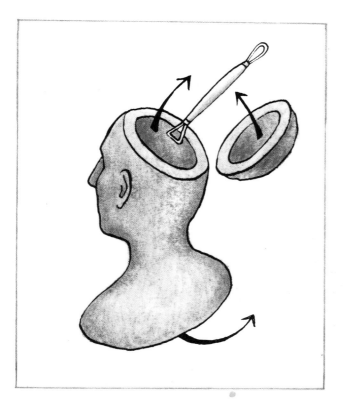

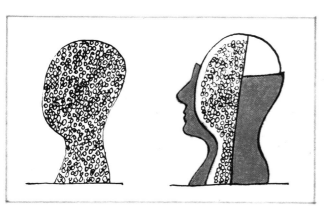

Fig. 66   Modelling a thin walled head. A core of wood wool or polystyrene is coated with a thin layer of plaster. Prior to modelling the plaster must be dressed with shellac to prevent it from absorbing water from the clay

Hand-building

In ceramic use, hand-building includes shaping or forming of figural work or hollow ware without a wheel or mould.

The greatest danger to be met in hand-building is represented by bubbles of air trapped in the batch. Therefore, utmost care should be taken to avoid bubbles forming from the very beginning, that is, when making a batch. The clay used should have low plasticity and possibly even be grogged. De-aeration is achieved by thorough pugging and wedging. The difficulty of working a nonplastic material will be more than outweighed by the relative safety of firing since any air which remains in the body regardless of how thorough the de-aeration can leave through the open, porous body.

Figural work is modelled without using an auxilliary core or only with cores that can easily be removed (fig. 66). Prior to firing the article must be cut into as many pieces as necessary for scooping all excess clay from the interior, leaving a body only as thick as required by the size and construction of the piece. Reinforcing ribs can be

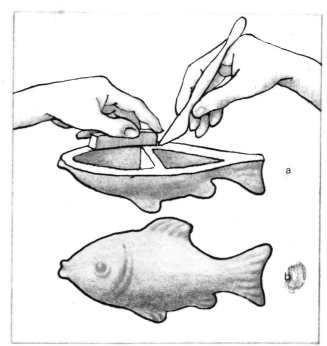

Fig. 67   Modelling hollow sculptures:
(a) The sculpture is hand-built from strips of clay luted together
(b) Finished article

left in places to prevent deformation during firing. To eliminate the danger of air bubbles, especially in plastic, non-porous (fat) clays, the body should be pierced all over with a nail or a fork but without quite reaching the surface. Pieces prepared in this way can then be reassembled and luted together with slip, the joints retouched or trimmed and, when the article is thoroughly dry, it can be fired.

Fig. 65 shows a head ready for firing. The top of the head is cut off and the clay is scooped from the inside. Piercing the body will ensure good de-aeration. The cut-off part is then roughened on the joint surface and luted to the body.

Another, truly ceramic technique is hollow modelling. Sculptures made in this way are not cut or scooped out afterwards but are built hollow from the very beginning, using thin strips of clay (fig. 67). Work produced in this way has a special character caused by combined modelling techniques. Large forms are pushed from the inside, small details are hand-modelled from the outside.

Figs 68-70 Modelling a jug

Fig. 68 Modelling a small jug from a ball of plastic clay

Fig. 69 The lip and handle are luted to the finished body

Fig. 70 The finished jug

HOLLOW WARE MODELLING

The simplest method of making hollow ware without a wheel is to form a bowl from a ball of clay by pressing one's thumb in it to make a hollow shape. The method is known as **pinching** and the wares as **pinchpots**. Using hands, spatulas or templates, the body is then given the desired shape and wall thickness. This age-old method, which can be used to produce hollow wares of surprising perfection and size, was not used only by primitive people but has survived in traditional pottery, for example, in Denmark where it is used to make the famous black smoked wares.

Fig. 71
(A) Modelling a vase using a template
(B) Trimming
(C) Smoothing the joint between two modelled and trimmed shapes that have been luted together

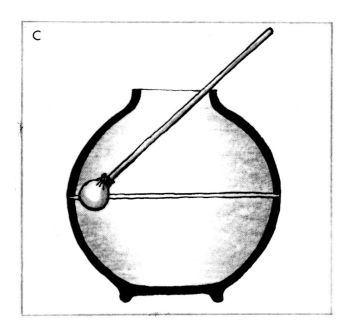

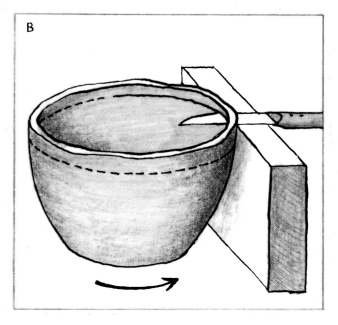

Another method, termed **coiling**, uses pencil-thick coils rolled from clay with which pots and even figures can be hand-built spirally. The surface of the built-up body can be smoothed with a spatula or the coiled structure can have a decorative function. One of the advantages of coiling is that if the coils are of uniform thickness, the body has a uniform wall.

Fig. 72 Preparing coils from soft, pliable clay. Coils made with spread fingers are more uniform in thickness than those rolled with the fingers pressed together

Fig. 73 Building a pot by luting coils together with slip

Fig. 74 A coiled plate, glazed and fired.

For coiling, extruded coils are made by forcing clay through a die by means of a simple piston-operated press or wad box. Wad boxes are also used to advantage to make profiled columns of clay known as wads which are then shaped to form handles.

Fig. 75 Schematic diagram of a piston-operated wad box. Various dies can be used to make all kinds of profiles and even pipes. Wad boxes are handy to make handles, spouts, applied decorations and kiln furniture

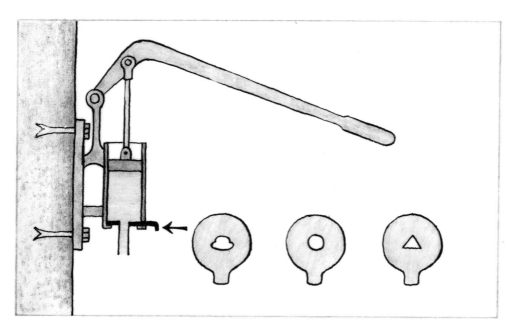

Fig. 76 Wad box used in the maiolica shop in Tupesy, Moravia. The piston is operated by a spoke wheel rather than a lever

The third method which deserves mention concerns making ceramic wares from **slabs**. The slabs are made as shown in the pictures, either by cutting slices off a block of clay using a harp bow, or rolled using a rolling pin. In both cases the slab thickness is determined by guide sticks (8-10 mm). For slab rolling special benches are marketed (fig. 79). Slabs can be used to build both pots and figures and even to line plaster moulds, that is for **press moulding**.

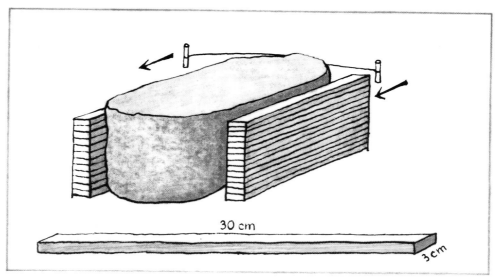

30 cm

3 cm

Fig. 77 Making a slab by slicing using guide sticks

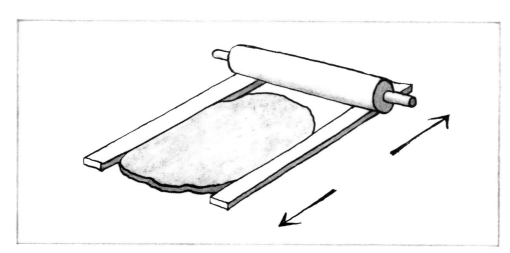

Fig. 78 Rolling a slab

123

Fig: 79 Slab rolling bench

Fig. 80 Cutting a clay slab into pieces

Fig. 82 A neck made from clay rings is luted to the finished slab vase

Fig. 81 Luting the pieces together with slip

Fig. 83 Finished vase

124

Throwing

Fig. 84   Traditional European throwing wheel

POTTER'S WHEEL

The potter's wheel is an invention dating back several thousand years. It originated from its predecessor, the potter's disc which was not mounted on a rotating shaft but turned by hand. A wheel mounted on a rigid rotating shaft appeared first in Babylonia during the 7th millennium BC. Research seems to show that Babylonia was the original home of the invention whose use then spread to Egypt in about 3000 BC and later also to India, Asia Minor, Crete and Greece. From Greece it reached Central Europe in about 500 BC.

The potter's wheel as it is used today does not differ much from those of the 18th century when wooden spoke wheels were replaced by iron discs and spindles.

The kickwheel used in Europe is composed of a vertical iron shaft bearing a small wheelhead on top. The wheelhead is usually made of iron, but may also be made of wood or plaster. At the bottom end of the shaft, a few centimetres above the ground, is mounted a large, heavy wooden, or more frequently iron, flywheel which gives the wheelhead sufficient momentum. The potter rotates the flywheel by friction, that is, by kicking his right sole forward, his left sole backward. The shaft is supported by two ball bearings, one located just under the wheelhead and set in the bench frame; the other is either embedded in the ground (thrust bearing, usually of the plain type), or is mounted on the bottom trestle of the bench (fig. 84).

Today, electrically driven throwing wheels are used. They come in various designs and sizes ranging from bench-mounted models to large units used for throwing tall wares at which the potter works standing (fig. 85).

Fig. 85   Power-driven potter's wheel

Fig. 86 Potter's tools:
Twisted wire with handles for cutting off the pot from the bat;
Potter's ribs (plumtree wood, biscuit, metal) used to shape the pot;
Handleless spoon and a piece of wood, both with fine smooth finish, for hollowing;
Swabstick and a halved wooden spoon for work inside pots with narrow neck;
Turning tools of various shapes for turning leather-hard wares;
Trimming knife

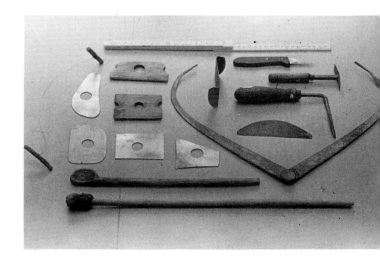

125

THROWING

Throwing, that is, building pots on a wheel using hands, is governed by specific rules. Although each potter has his own system and skills, the procedure is essentially always the same (figs 87-109).

Figure 88: The rotating ball of clay is pressed hard dead centre with both hands. This operation, which is called centering, is vital for the whole throwing process.

Figure 89: The ball is shaped by hand into a thick-walled bowl. By pressing the thumbs against the bottom it gains the correct thickness.

Figure 87: A lump of the required size is cut from a block of well-wedged clay and made into a ball. The quantity of clay is either estimated, or, in the case of repetitious throwing, the clay is weighed. The ball is placed in the centre of the bat and the wheel is set in motion. Note that the hands must be kept permanently wet while working.

Figure 90: The bowl is now pulled up, forming a cone. Coning produces the basic shape which is then modified by pressing down and out to make bowls and dishes or alternatively, by pulling up to make tall pots.

Figure 91: Pulling the cone taller.

Figure 92: Another way of pulling the body up and making the wall thinner.

Figure 93: The pot is now wider and the wall is formed using a rib.

Figure 94: Shaping the pot by hand and a rib.

Figure 95: Forming the jug lip.

Figure 96: Cutting the finished jug from the bat with a wire.

Figure 97: The principle of good throwing is to maintain a uniform thickness of the wall at every stage of the operation. Only the rim should be left thicker to provide spare material to throw from.

Figure 98: Narrow-necked pots where the hand cannot reach inside are thrown with the help of a stick tipped with a cloth ball (see fig. 86).

Bowl or dish-shaped wares — in this particular case a dish — are made in the same manner as described above as far as the coning stage.

Figure 99: The cone is now pressed and at the same time pulled wider.

Figure 100: The wall is pulled higher and wider using a rib.

Figure 101: Further use of a rib.

Figures 102, 103: Removing the dish from the wheel. As described above, the finished article is cut off but if there is a risk of the article being deformed, another method is used: larger wares are thrown on a plaster bat fixed to the wheelhead. The finished article is not cut off but the bat is lifted off the wheelhead together with the article. There are also special mechanical ejector bats available.

The two examples of throwing illustrated above have been selected to show the principles of simple throwing of tall and wide articles. However, the wheel can also be used to throw more complicated wares, for example, big garden pots. These are thrown in several separate pieces which are then luted together when leather-hard and turned to shape. Large wares are usually thrown by two people, one rotating the wheel, the other doing the throwing.

Pots with spouts are likewise assembled from two separate pieces, as the spout is thrown from a tube, given the desired shape and then luted to the body.

An interesting procedure is the throwing of a **Kugelhopf** baking mould:

Figure 106: Decorative fluting is made with wet fingers pressed in the still soft body.

Figure 104: In the centre of a flamened ball of clay a tall cone is thrown. This will be the contre of the baking mould.

Figure 107: The final operation involves luting the handles to the body.

Figure 105: Around the centre the mould wall is thrown.

Most thrown wares are trimmed when leather-hard, or turned. Trimming is used to finish the bottom to which the foot is to be luted. Then the entire surface of the pot is trimmed. Turning on vertical or horizontal lathes is used to finish mainly technical wares but turning may also be used to obtain pots with a thin wall. For example, Josiah Wedgwood used to have his wares turned to one-third of the original wall thickness.

Trimming procedures can be seen from the following pictures:

Figure 108: The bottom of the dish is trimmed with a tool and the place where the foot is to be luted is made rougher. A clay column — the future foot — is luted with slip.

Figure 109: Throwing the foot by hand and with a natural sponge.
For moulding methods see figures 110-113.

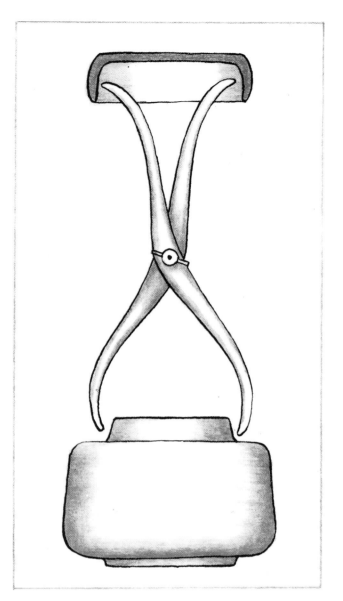

Fig. 110   Combination inside and outside calipers for measuring pots

Fig. 111   Scalloping a rim

Jigger and jolley

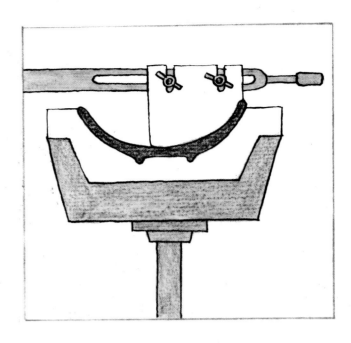

Pots produced on a large scale are rarely thrown by hand but moulded on a machine known as a jigger and jolley, that is, a power-driven wheel bearing a plaster mould and having a movable arm equipped with a metal tool, in fact, a template or die. Deep pots, namely bowls, vases, etc., are moulded in rotating hollow moulds, with the arm shaping the inside. Plates and dishes are thrown on convex formers while the jolley arm shapes the underside.

Deep vessels are shaped from a ball of clay thrown into the mould (fig. 113). To make a plate, a separate slab is made first on another jigger.

Fig. 113   Jiggering a dish

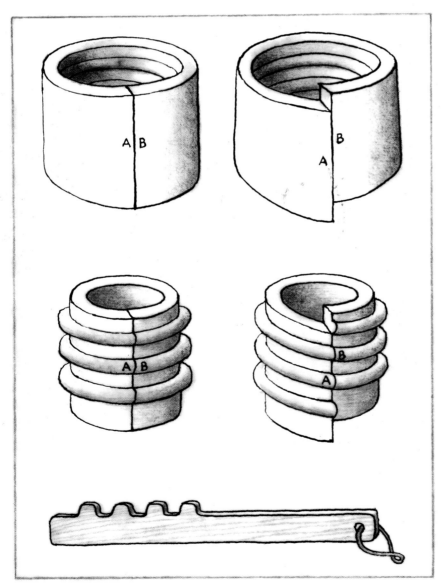

Fig. 112   Throwing a helix according to a book by C. Piccolpasso (1573)

132

It is then pressed on to the mould former using a wetted sponge and the jolley arm with the die is brought on to it to give it shape (figs 114-117).

Narrow-necked pots are thrown using a hand-held die or on machines using an excentric jolley arm which is movable.

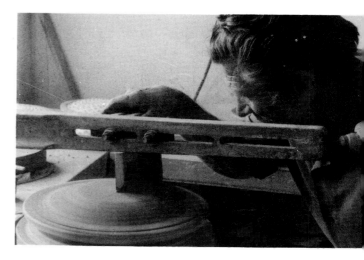

Fig. 116   Using a wooden template to make the underside of a dish

Fig. 114   Jigger and jolley with a former for an openwork dish

Fig. 117   Cutting openwork of jiggered dishes

Fig. 115   A clay slab is pressed on to the former moistened with a sponge

Hand-shaping

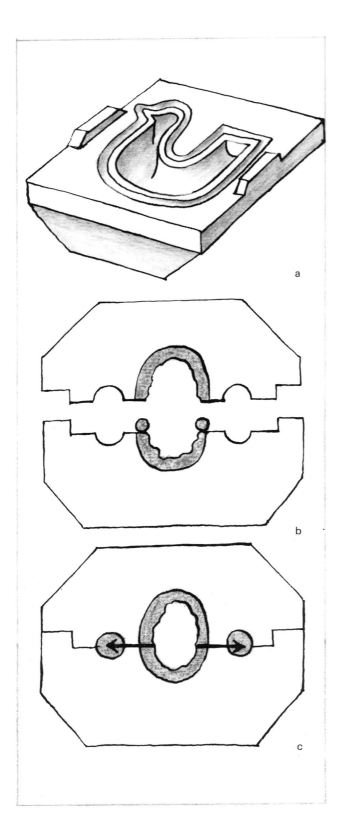

Other methods of shaping ceramic products include **slip casting** and **press moulding**.

Press moulding by hand is used mostly for modelled ceramics. Plastic clay is pressed into the mould carefully to take even the minutest of details. Care must be taken to drive all air bubbles out. The joints of the individually moulded pieces are scored, smeared with slip and luted by pressing them together. Excess slip leaves via outlets. Press mouldings is shown schematically in fig. 118.

The technique is also used for making sprigs, that is, flat reliefs of the sort used typically for Wedgwood wares.

Bernard Leach describes an interesting technique used by Chinese potters for making dishes and plates decorated with reliefs. The plates were shaped on convex biscuit formers bearing a negative relief (fig. 119). The potter then blew through a hole cut in the bottom to separate the finished plate from the former. Dishes with relief decorations used to be made in a similar way by the Habaner in Moravia and Slovakia.

The same principle involving convex formers is also used to make pastry moulds. Two examples can be seen in figs 120-122.

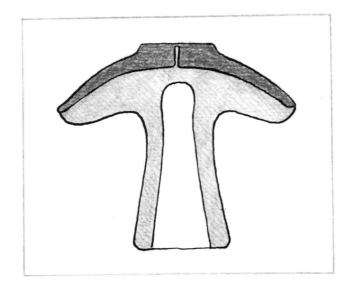

Fig. 118 *Schematic diagram showing hand-pressing (press moulding):*
(a) One half of the mould with a duct taking in surplus clay
(b) Sectional view of a mould prepared for pressing
(c) Sectional view of a closed mould; surplus clay has been forced into the ducts

Fig. 119 *Chinese biscuit former for making dishes by hand. The elongated bottom part of the former serves as a handle*

XXIV
Vase
Otto Eckert, Czechoslovakia, 1980
Stoneware, blue slip, matt transparent glaze,
decoration produced with wooden mallets; electric
kiln, 1200 °C. Height 55 cm. Private collection

XXV
Early Morning Jump
Šárka Radová, Czechoslovakia, 1980
Porcelain with overglaze painting; oil fired at 1380 °C
Height 45 cm
Private collection

XXVI
Blossoms in Landscape
Jindřiška Radová, Czechoslovakia, 1983
Porcelain decorated with wax technique and white, ferruginous and celadon glazes; oil fired, reducing atmosphere, 1320 °C
Diameter 40 cm
Private collection

BEATING CLAY INTO MOULDS

This is a technique used in making tiles. Stiff clay is beaten into wooden moulds with wooden beaters or plungers to give the clay compactness. Chinese unglazed stoneware products such as a teapot shown on illustration 23 are manufactured from tiles made this way.

XXVII ▶
Pair
Klaus Schultze, West Germany, 1983
Composed of high-fired bricks tooled with diamond saw, some parts glazed and fired electrically at lower temperature
280 × 160 × 110 cm
Skulpturenstrasse Asamhof, Munich

138

Slip casting

Fig. 120   Biscuit pastry mould

Slip casting is one of the youngest ceramic shaping techniques. It originated in the early 19th century in Sèvres, France, but became widespread only at the end of the last century when a physician named Götz, from Carlsbad, Bohemia, had a patent issued in his name for deflocculation of the casting slip with soda. Slip casting is used for making complicated figural work since the slip penetrates even very minute details of the mould.

Casting slip is prepared from clay by adding water and soda, water glass or another liquefying agent (deflocculant). In practice, any liquid clay is called slip but technical literature distinguishes **water slip**, that is, clay liquefied only by water, from **casting slip**, that is, clay which is made liquid by adding a small quantity of water with some deflocculant. The difference and effect in manufacture is considerable. To make clay liquid by adding merely water, some 60-80 per cent of the latter are required, while casting slips contain only 20-40 per cent water. Besides, moulds used for casting with water slip can be used only two or three times without drying while those used for casting with casting slip can be re-used up to 10-15 times.

Deflocculants include soda (1-2 g soda per 1000 g dry clay), water glass, sodium aluminate, sodium phosphate and humic acid. There are also various commercial deflocculants marketed under various brand names. It is necessary to test which and how much deflocculant your clay needs.

Fig. 122   Templates for hand making profiles of ceramic tiles

Fig. 121   Biscuit pastry mould

Sometimes several must be combined to produce the desired effect.

Air bubbles cause problems in slip casting. It is, therefore, recommended to avoid mixing the slip rapidly or jerkily or pouring it from any height, otherwise the slip would foam and form bubbles. To prevent clots from entering the mould, it is advisable to pour the slip through a lawn, that is a coarse-mesh sieve with at least 16 openings per square centimetre.

carefully stirred to drive out air bubbles. The moulds are left for some time to allow the plaster to absorb water. When a thick enough layer of clay has formed on the walls of the moulds, excess slip is poured off.

Figure 125: Using a piece of soft clay the riser is removed to allow easy pouring of surplus slip.

Figure 123: Slip casting is illustrated below, using an example of a cat figurine cast in three separate pieces (illustrated above).

Figure 124: The slip is poured in the moulds and

Figure 126: When the casts are hard enough to be removed, they are stuck together with slip and retouched; for comparison, see the finished cat decorated with decals (lithographic transfers).

DECORATION TECHNIQUES

Figs 127, 128   Luting a handle

The techniques of ceramic decoration can be divided into two large categories, that is, modelling and painting. Naturally, the two complement each other and cannot, therefore, be strictly separated. It is difficult to tell whee one ends and the other begins and every ceramic artist, whether he considers himself more of a painter or a sculptor, must have a command of both.

Decoration techniques discussed in this book may, of course, be combined, for example, sgraffito with painting, or engraving with stamping and slip (engobe).

However, not all techniques described here are suited to studio work. Some remain almost exclusively limited to industrial manufacture but every creative artist should be familiar with them in order to be able to design wares made industrially.

Besides cast handles shown in fig. 50, there are also coiled (rolled), extruded and pulled handles. Rolled handles are made from rolled coils, bent to shape and luted with slip to the body which should have the same rigidity as the handle. The joint is retouched. Extruded handles are made from profiled pieces of clay extruded on a wad box (fig. 75) and then luted in the same way. An interesting method is pulling a handle (fig. 127). A clay coil is dipped in slip at one end and luted to the body in the top joint. When the joint is firm, the potter uses his wet hands to pull the coil between his fingers to give it the required length and profile (figs 127 and 128). The handle is then bent to shape and the bottom end of the coil dipped in slip and luted to the body. When dry, the handle is retouched.

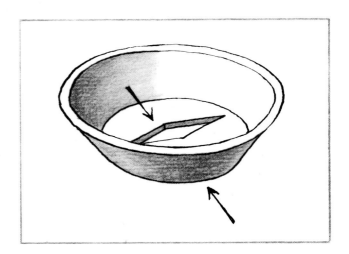

Fig. 129   Making a round dish into an oval one

Techniques of plastic decoration

SHAPING

If we disregard the fact that the perfect shape of a body in itself is the foremost element of decoration, the first decoration technique which comes to mind is shaping the soft pot on the wheel or the pot which has just been removed from the mould. The only tools required for this purpose are wet hands and a natural sponge (fig. 109).

When the body is still touch-dry but pliable, it can be further shaped by various means. For example, a round vase can be beaten to shape with a flat wooden paddle or a hard rubber mallet. If a paddle with a grooved or scored surface is used, it will give the body a decorative finish. Fig. 129 shows how a round dish is made into an oval one. A piece is carved out from the bottom as required, the joints are pressed together to see if the shape is correct, scored and luted with slip. The raised rim is trimmed level.

a

44 (a, b)
Shishi Lion
Kyoto, Japan, 19th century
Brown stoneware decorated with fine engraving (fur), partially glazed
20 × 23 cm
Private collection

b

APPLIED DECORATIONS

Applied decorations constitute one of the oldest and most widespread categories of decoration techniques used in all kinds of ceramic wares (fig. 130). The range of decorations is very wide, ranging from a simple coil luted on to a pot to fine bas-relief sprigs of Wedgwood ware.

Reliefs modelled by hand or press moulded by hand in plaster or biscuit moulds are luted to partially dry but still plastic bodies. The decoration should be of approximately the same density as the body. The reverse of the sprig is scored and luted to the body with slip and then retouched. Folk potters of the past used an interesting method to make hair and fur for their figurines by forcing a thin paste through a cloth or sieve. The strands were then applied to pottery figurines.

Fig. 130   Decorating a porcelain vase with luted sprigs

45
Candle box
Prachatice district, south Bohemia, first half of 19th century
Unglazed pottery; luted openwork strips used to reinforce walls serve as decoration
38 × 11.5 × 48 cm
Municipal Museum, Prachatice, Czechoslovakia
(Research data by courtesy of Vladimír Scheufler)

46
Tankard
Altenburg, Germany, 1713
Stoneware with brown glaze, decorated with white stamped relief and quartz pebble pattern, pewter trimming. Height 28 cm
Museum of Decorative Arts, Prague

STAMPING

Another very old decoration technique involves impressing the body surface with negative reliefs. For this purpose, various metal, plaster, biscuit or wooden stamping tools may be used (figs 131 to 133). Impressions must be made into a relatively soft clay to prevent cracking of the body. On the other hand, the body must be solid enough to prevent sticking of the stamp and deformation under pressure.

Rouletting is impressing the body with wheels or rolls bearing a pattern. Roulettes may be of metal, plaster or biscuit. As the roulette revolves around its axis held in a handle, it imprints the pattern into the body, forming strips of regularly repeated design (figs 131, 132).

Note that plaster roulettes should have metal hubs to accommodate the axle because plaster is highly susceptible to wear.

Fig. 132 Roulettes

Fig. 131 Relief stamp

INCISION TECHNIQUES

The most widely used technique for decorating raw bodies is incision, distinguished by the width of the cut into engraving, grooving and fluting.

All three methods require pure, smooth bodies with no coarse-grained impurities. Various pointed tools are used, some of which are shown in fig. 134. Metal tools with a sharp point are better for dry, hard bodies, while wooden chisel-like tools are suitable for softer bodies as they remove the clay easily and do not leave sharp, untrimmed cuts. Chinese and Korean potters use bamboo

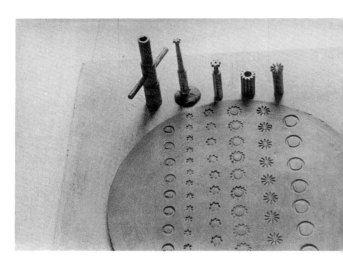

Fig. 133 Various objects can be used for stamping

tools, usually pointed at both ends. There are also combing tools.

Fig. 134 g shows a fluting plane (dado plane) used by Chinese potters. The blade is a thin piece of metal; sometimes it may be serrated at the edge.

47 ▶
Headrest
China, 12th century
Tz' chou yao stoneware, brownish body with white slip and engraved decoration
14 × 28 × 16 cm
National Gallery, Prague

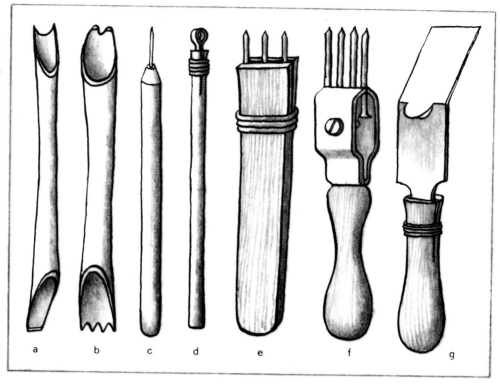

Fig. 134   Some tools for engraving raw clay:
(a, b) Bamboo tools
(c) Metal pointed tool
(d) Steel palette made from a watch spring
(e, f) Metal combs
(g) Metal dado plane

48
Dish
Perugia, Italy, 1500-1520
Mezzomaiolica with decoration engraved in white slip
and painted blue, yellow and violet
Diameter 38 cm
Museum of Decorative Arts, Prague

INLAY AND CHROMOLITH

The negative trace produced by incision or stamping can be used as a starting point for yet another decoration technique, that is ceramic **inlaying.**
The incisions are carefully filled with engobes (slips) of a colour different from that of the body and the pot is left to dry slowly to allow the body and the decoration to obtain the same solidity. To prevent cracking, inlay pastes must contain some non-plastic material such as kaolin, quartz or fireclay.

When leather-hard, the inlay is shaved level with the body using a razor blade.

Chromolith is a term used for inlays in hard unglazed stoneware.

OPENWORK AND FACETING

Openwork and cutting of facets are also common techniques used to decorate semi-dry bodies.

In openwork, the ornament is first cut out roughly with a sharp thin knife. When the body is dry, details of the pattern are repaired and sharp edges rounded with a sponge (fig. 117). Recently laser equipment has been introduced for making openwork ornaments. No stencils are required because the pattern is traced by a computer-stored programme.

The same technique was also used for double pots (ill. 49). The inner body was solid, while the outer pot was made with basket or lace-like openwork ornament.

The other method consists of cutting facets on round bodies. In fact, it is an extension of the shaping techniques discussed earlier. The places where faceting is to be made are thrown or built thicker. Smooth facets are best made with a knife, textured ones with profiled tools. A small draw-knife (barking iron) is also very helpful.

Sharply curving bodies are best formed first with a paddle or maller (see Shaping) and only then faceted with a knife.

PÂTE-SUR-PÂTE

This porcelain decoration technique originated in China but was successfully perfected in Sèvres, France, from where it spread to many European porcelain factories. Using a dark biscuit or glost-fired body, a fine bas-relief of clay slip is applied with a brush. The slip is applied successively in thin layers, always when the preceding one has dried. The finished relief is smoothed by modelling tools. To facilitate work, the slip is mixed with a bit of gum arabic or tragacanth.

The body is then glazed with a translucent glaze and fired. The dark body shows through the thin relief, producing subtle transitions of light and shadow.

49
Teapot
Japan, 17th-18th century
Brown stoneware, double body decorated with openwork and rich relief ornamentation
Height 11 cm
Museum of Decorative Arts, Prague

147

a

50 (a, b)
Odalisque
Slavkov (Schlaggenwald),
Bohemia, 3rd quarter of
19th century
Porcelain lithophane
(negative and positive
views)
Length 18.5 cm
Museum of Decorative
Arts, Prague

b

LITHOPHANE

As in the case of *pâte-sur-pâte*, **lithophane** produces painting-like effects by plastic means. The porcelain body is thinned according to a design to produce a translucent pattern or even scene distinguished by several intensities of translucence when viewed against light (page 148, ill. 50).

The design is first made in a wax plate of the same thickness and translucence as the body to be cast. The wax plate is held against light while working to facilitate control of translucence. The finished wax relief (which has different proportions from normal reliefs) is then cast in plaster to produce a mould which is used to make a porcelain body of the same thickness as the wax plate.

PORCELAIN LACE

Lace on porcelain vases or figurines is made from real lace dipped in slip mixed with some adhesive. The thin slip fills the openings in the lace and must, therefore, be removed with a needle prior to firing. When fired, the lace incinerates and the vase receives its imprint in porcelain (fig. 135). Fired lace is extremely fine and brittle and even a slight pressure applied during glazing may damage it. Only when fired will the lace have sufficient strength (fig. 136).

Needless to say, only cotton lace is suitable for this type of work, since nylon and other plastic materials melt and disintegrate in fire.

Fig. 135   Arranging lace on a porcelain vase

Fig. 136   A vase ready for biscuit firing. Next to it a finished vase

Painting techniques

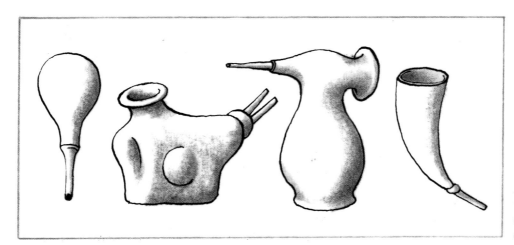

Fig. 137 Rubber bulb, clay slip trailers and trailing horn

Fig. 138 Slip trailing with
(A) trailer
(B) rubber bulb

SLIP DECORATION

Prior to applying **slip** (sometimes also known as **engobe**, especially in the USA), it is necessary to test the body material to prevent peeling and shivering. The best way is to use a leather-hard body. Some bodies require moistening with a sponge prior to slip application, other batches will stand slipping on a thoroughly dry surface.

The simplest ways of slip application include **dipping**, **pouring** and **spraying**. The procedure is practically the same as with glazing (see figs 15-23), but work with slips is more difficult and requires more experience. The application must be performed rapidly to prevent slip water from penetrating the body. It will be found that errors are difficult to correct.

SLIP TRAILING

Slip trailers or tracers are a very old invention indeed. Their design may vary but they are used all over Europe as well as elsewhere. They are usually small pottery containers glazed on the inside, sometimes also on the outside. The container has two holes, one for filling, the other used for the application of slip on the body. The trailing nozzle is inset with a finely sharpened quill (of a diameter ranging from 1 to 2 mm) and held in place with a piece of cork or clay. In some places an ox horn is used instead, but a rubber bulb tipped with a syringe can also be used to advantage because, by applying pressure on the bulb with fingers, it is possible to control the outflow (figs 137, 138). The slip trailer is used either to paint with or to produce run slip decoration or

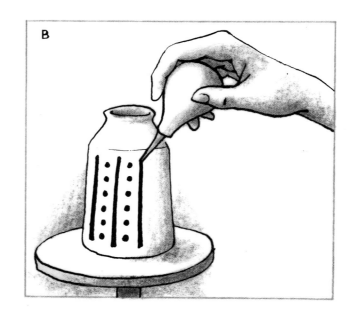

Fig. 139 Clay slip trailers (from the collection of H. Landsfeld)

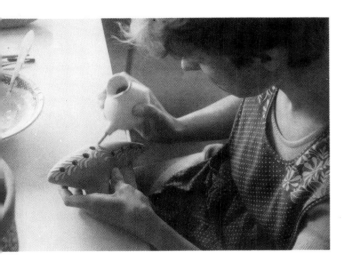

Fig. 140 Decorating an ocarina with slip trailer

Fig. 141 Dribbling slip with a trailer

marbling effects. Pigment paints and glazes may be used but the practice is to use slips.

When working with a slip trailer, the left hand holds the pot which should be slightly inclined. The right hand holds the trailer filled with a well-mixed colour or slip. The quill tip is lightly tapped against the pot and the trailer is tilted until the colour starts flowing and one can start painting. Note that the quill must never lose contact with the body (fig. 140). Slip trailing is relatively difficult and requires much skill and a light touch.

In Czech, the slip trailer is known as a 'cuckoo'. The name comes from the sound the trailer gives when shaken prior to work. The pictures show slip trailing using a trailer, as well as slip trailers of several types.

Fig. 142 Jerking will make the trailed slip penetrate the base slip

151

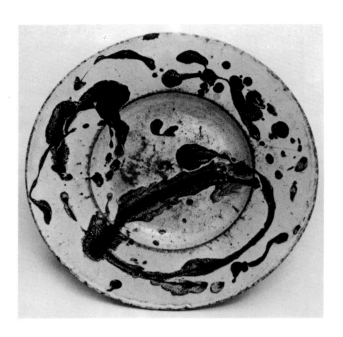

51
Plate
Bohemia, 18th century
Faience with blue trailed slip
Diameter 33 cm
Ethnographical Museum, Prague

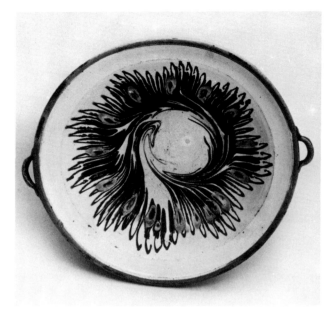

52
Dish
Modra, Slovakia, early 20th century
Pottery, white slip with blue and light brown trailed
slip, transparent glaze. Diameter 27.5 cm
Ethnographical Museum, Prague

53
Dish
South Bohemia, early 18th century
Pottery, blue glaze with white marbling
Diameter 28 cm
Ethnographical Museum, Prague

54
Dish
South Bohemia, early 18th century
Pottery, blue glaze with white trailed slip
Diameter 28 cm
Ethnographical Museum, Prague

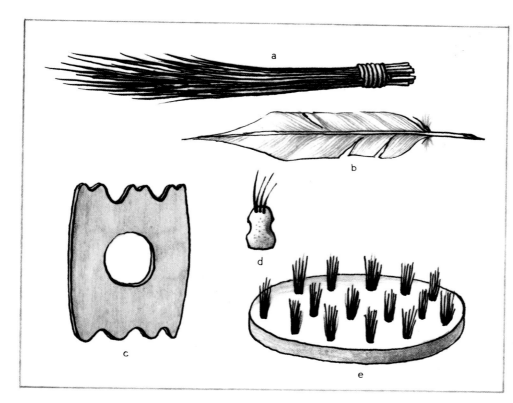

Fig. 143 Tools used for slip trailing and marbling: (a) wicker brush, (b) feather, (c) leather or rubber comb, (d) hare's whiskers, (e) a traditional marbling tool used by Slovak potters

Fig. 144 Folk tool for dabbing with slip

RUN SLIPS AND MARBLING

Some very interesting and old slip decoration techniques are the so-called run slips and marbling. A leather-hard dish is dipped in a basic slip to produce a relatively thick coat. Then, before the slip coat can solidify, another slip of contrasting colour is dribbled on the surface using a trailer (fig. 141). The nozzle is held about 1 cm above the surface. The density of the trailed slip must be the same as that of the dip slip to produce a uniform surface. Naturally, it is also possible to use several slips of different colour. When the dribbling is finished, the dish is held in both hands and jerked sideways or given a sharp twist. Alternatively, the dish may be placed on a small board resting on a projection and tilted to and fro. In both cases the coloured trails will penetrate each other and the basic slip will rise to the surface, forming a fine hairline pattern (fig. 142).

According to H. Landsfeld, Slovak potters used to improve their run slips with hare's whiskers set in a piece of biscuit (fig. 143). The whisker tips, immersed slightly in the wet marble slip, produced various hairline ornaments when the tool was jerked to and fro. A feather cut to form a long point was also used for this purpose, hence the term **feathering** (fig. 143.)

The methods described above are used mainly for decorating dishes and plates. In deep pots, the slip is dribbled on the rim and left to run down freely. At an appropriate moment the pot is tilted and simultaneously twisted so that the slip trails produce a coloured spiral ornament.

If the colour or slip is mixed with an extract of tobacco or with hydrogen peroxide rather than water, the running slip produces a fantastic lace-like dendritic pattern, but glycerine, soapy water, oil, water glass, soda and other materials will also produce all kinds of unusual ornaments.

Marbling can also be produced by another method. The basic slip is poured into a large, wide pot and a contrasting slip is dribbled on top of it. The dish to be marbled is dipped in the place where the coloured drops float on the surface and quickly pulled out. The sharp movement mixes the two slips, producing an interesting marbled pattern.

153

Fig. 145   Dabbing tools: cloth pads and natural sponge

Fig. 146   Decorating an article with a sponge

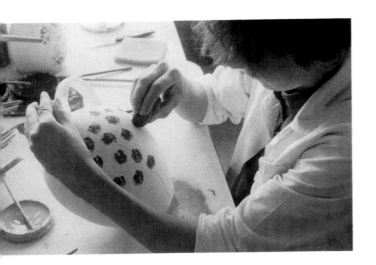

SLIP COMBING

Slightly wet slips can also be decorated with a soft rubber or leather combing tool with rounded tips, a fine wicker brush (fig. 143) or hard bristle brushes cut to various shapes. The tools impress a fine relief trace in the slip, or the slip can be removed right to the body surface.

STENCILS

Decorating with the aid of stencils is a very old Oriental technique, used for instance by potters of the Sung period. A positive or negative stencil is laid on the surface or even glued to it with starch or sugar water. The body is then dipped in slip or sprayed with a colour or a glaze. When the coat is dry, the stencil is carefully removed.

This technique requires working with large masses of simple shapes which can be further decorated by engraving, coloured contours, etc. Chinese potters used stencils made from paper or plant leaves, but today thin metal foils are used to advantage.

Stencil decorations can be applied to all types of ceramic wares, either under the glaze, on the raw glaze or the fired glaze.

DABBING

This is another age-old ceramic decoration technique. Colour is applied to a body or a glaze with a piece of natural sponge, cotton pad, a tuft of wood wool or any other suitable material giving the body an interesting surface structure (figs 145, 146).

Dabbing can be used to advantage if a large area is to be covered with a coat of colour and no spray gun is available. In such a case the colour is applied on a fired glaze with a fine, wide paintbrush and dabbed with a soft pad. To inhibit drying, a small quantity of clove oil may be added to the colour.

UNDERGLAZE PAINTING

Decoration of once-fired bodies with underglaze colours, glazes or salt solutions is termed underglaze painting.

Underglaze colours are usually thinned with water with a small quantity of tragacanth or some other glue added to prevent washing off the applied decoration when the body is dipped in glaze. Turpentine, balsam or other similar substances may also be used but whenever oily or resinous thinners are used the body must be slightly fired prior to glazing to ensure that the glaze adheres evenly to the body. Underglaze painting on open bodies has much in common with watercolour painting: it must be done rapidly and no retouching is possible. Thick layers of colour are to be avoided to inhibit shattering and peeling of the glaze and other defects.

If the design is too intricate to permit rapid working, the body should be rendered nonabsorbent by impregnating it with various substances like gum arabic, soft soap, wax dissolved in turpentine, etc. In such cases the colours are

XXVIII
Fan Form
Karl Scheid, West Germany, 1983
Porcelain with relief decoration, feldspathic glaze;
reduction fired in a gas kiln at 1360 °C
17.5 × 13 × 3.7 cm
Private collection

XXIX
Vases
Elly and Wilhelm Kuch, West Germany, 1984
Partially glazed and painted stoneware; gas fired at
1320 °C
Height 29 and 26 cm
Private collection

XXX
Elevåtion
Lewis D. Snyder, USA, 1984
Stoneware decorated with glazes; gas kiln, reducing
atmosphere, 1285 °C
Diameter 75 cm
Private collection

XXXI
Still Life with Box and Doll
Marta Taberyová, Czechoslovakia, 1985
Stoneware with fireclay and porcelain decorated with
pigment oxides, gold and platinum; oxidation fired
at 1280 °C
55 × 55 cm
Private collection

mixed with resinous substances, for example turpentine, balsam, etc., and the body must be slightly fired before glazing.

More details on underglaze colours are given on pages 86, 87.

The design to be painted can be outlined in indelible pencil, which will burn out in the firing. For repeated motifs stencils can be made from parchment paper or tinfoil with the outline perforated with a needle. The perforated stencil is then laid against the body and dusted with graphite which penetrates through the perforation and traces the pattern on the body (fig. 147).

Instead of colours, low-melting glazes may be used for painting, but these must be applied in thicker layers. The resulting effect is softer, since it is fused into a transparent overglaze.

However, if high-melting glazes are used for underglaze painting, they will not fuse with the overglaze but instead will remain under the latter as a fine relief.

Salt solutions which also are essentially underglaze colours have been discussed in detail in the chapter dealing with colours, see page 87.

55
Milk cooler
Kralovice, Bohemia, 1870—90
Pottery, brown glaze, white marbling
Height 19 cm
Municipal Museum, Kralovice, Czechoslovakia
(Research data by courtesy of Vladimír Scheufler)

DRAWING WITH PASTELS

Pastels for drawing on unglazed biscuit bodies are marketed commercially but the studio artist can easily make them himself.

A solution of about 20 g gum arabic and 1 litre water is prepared, the exact quantity of the gum depending on the required hardness of the pastel.

Bone glue, gelatine or casein may also be used.

Using a glass muller, a thin paste is made from the solution and powdered kaolin or white clay and stained with a pigment oxide or stain. The coloured mixture is then rolled into sticks and wrapped in adhesive-coated paper and left to dry.

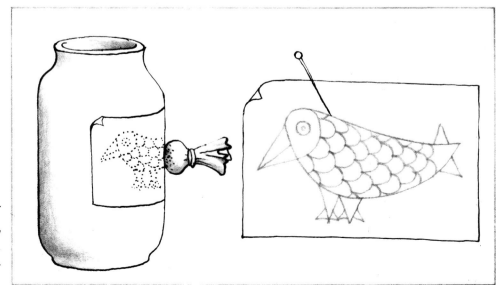

Fig. 147 Parchment paper or tinfoil template. The contours are pierced with a pin, the pad is filled with graphite or powdered coal

Drawing with these pastels or crayons is the same as with those used on paper. Excess pastel powder must be blown off from the surface to prevent it from fusing with the glaze.

BISCUIT ENGRAVING

Another underglaze decoration technique involves engraving of fired biscuit with dry point burins. The engraved body is then given a thin coating of underglaze colour which fills the engraved lines. The coloured coat on the uncut smooth surface can either be worked with a sponge to produce fine shading, combined with painting or washed clean.

SGRAFFITO

The same tools as in the last case can be used to scratch a coat of colour, glaze or slip to reveal the body, usually biscuit-fired, underneath. If several coats of different colour are used, multicoloured sgraffito designs can be produced.

The same method is used to scratch dry but unfired colours in fired glazes. On-glaze colours can be scratched with sharp, chisel-like wooden or bamboo tools.

PAINTING IN RAW GLAZE

The method of painting into raw glazes has already been discussed in the chapter dealing with colours, see page 89.

Figure 148 shows painting a vase covered with raw glaze. The vase is on a whirler which permits rotation of the body.

PAINTING ON FIRED GLAZE

Painting on fired glaze is done with on-glaze colours, lustre colours, low-melting enamels and precious metals. Details concerning these materials and their use can be found in the chapter dealing with colours.

Wax pastels or aniline colours mixed with glue

56
Wave Variation — Ripple, dish
Eileen Lewenstein, England, 1983
White stoneware with dark blue and pale green slip and drawing in black pastel; electrically fired at 1245 °C
Private collection

57
Plate
Jindřichův Hradec district,
Bohemia, 1693
Mezzomaiolica, buff body,
blue slip, engraved
decoration, transparent
glaze
Diameter 28 cm
Ethnographical Museum,
Prague

Fig. 148   Painting in raw glaze

can be used to sketch the design on to a fired glaze.

Large areas which would be difficult to paint with a brush are first coated with a mixture of turpentine and balsam. The coat is left to dry and then dusted with ground pigment. The thickness of the colour layer depends on how dry the coat is, since a wet base will absorb more pigment than a dry one, producing richer or paler shades, respectively. Dabbing may also be used (see page 154).

BANDING

Banding is used for underglaze, in-glaze and on-glaze decoration. The materials include slips, colours and metals. Banding is applied either as the only decorative element or it may be combined with other techniques. It can be done on regular wheels or on special desk-mounted devices known as **whirlers** or **banding wheels** (fig. 149). The article is placed dead centre on the wheel, the elbow of the right arm is pressed firmly against one's body, the tip of a brush or trailer touching the surface lightly. Banding is produced by rotating the article. Large factories generally use automatic banding machines.

Fig. 149 *Dish banding*

Fig. 150 *Spraying a saucer with a resist varnish*

RESIST TECHNIQUES

Any part of the body which is not to be coloured can be protected by the so-called **resist**. One possibility is to use stencils (fig.149) which constitute a related technique and have been discussed earlier. Resist techniques proper involve coating the body or its parts with an impervious substance which must be easily removable.

Fired glazes can be treated with a thick solution of gum arabic, biscuit or leather-hard surfaces with a paste made from kaolin and starch or dextrin. When the applied colour is dry, the protective coat is removed: gum arabic is simply washed off with water since on-glaze colours are insoluble in water, while the mixture of kaolin and glue can be easily blown off with a stream of air when dry. Greasy resists made from a mixture of wax, printer's ink and turpentine must be removed by firing.

The industry uses **resist varnishes**. **Acetone varnish** is used to cover the entire body, using a brush or dipping. The areas to be coloured are then cut out of the varnish layer using an electric needle (fig. 152), either by hand or using a template. **Alcohol varnishes** are used either for painting or for covering entire areas with a brush. After the article is sprayed with colour, the remaining varnish must be removed as soon as possible, using a sharp knife (figs 150, 151). Too hard a colour would peel and the contours could be damaged.

It is also possible to use a positive transfer varnish sprayed with a gun or applied onto transfer paper by means of silk screen printing. The desired motif is cut out from the paper and trans-

Fig. 151 *After spraying, the varnish coat is removed with a knife*

ferred on to the body as in decalcomania (see page 167). The transfer varnisch can be removed either immediately after the colour has been sprayed on the body, or when the colour is dry, since the resist coat can be washed off with water.

The composition of resist materials will be found in the recipe section (page 173).

An old Oriental technique is wax resist. The decoration is drawn on the body with a hot mixture of three parts wax and one part paraffin oil. The oil is very important as it prevents peeling of the wax when cold. The mixture is applied with a brush or a batik needle. The wax resist method is used mostly on biscuit or on glazed but unfired bodies, over which another coat of glaze is applied by dipping or spraying. The places covered with wax resist retain the colour of the base when the body is fired.

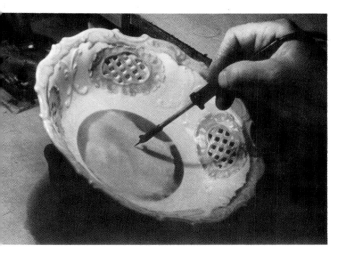

Drawing of the body may also be done with a candle or with wax crayons. Both may also be used for drawing on fired glaze; they have good resist properties and produce a trace of a different character to melted wax.

Larger surfaces may also be covered with an emulsion of wax and water (for example, various wood-impregnating emulsions), but these substances are suitable only for fired porous wares.

CLOISONNÉ ENAMEL

This type of decoration is found on old Chinese pottery and porcelain. Thin clay strips are luted to an unfired, leather-hard body, forming tiny partitions (hence the French term). The body is then glazed and fired and afterwards the partitions are filled with coloured enamels.

The technique is similar to that used for metal enamel work.

PAINTING BRUSHES

In the past, every potter used to make his own painting brushes from the hair of domestic and wild animals. The common materials included hare's whiskers, hair from the inside of ox ears and pig bristle. The long and very flexible hare's whiskers were placed in the centre and surrounded by pig bristle, while the periphery of the brush was formed by ox hair. The number of hair types as well as their quantity differed according to the purpose for which the brush was used.

Thin, long brushes made from hare's whiskers were used for contour work; thicker ones containing more hair were used for banding. A brush

Fig. 152 Cutting acetone varnish with an electric needle

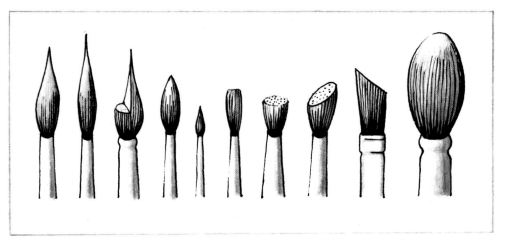

Fig. 153 A selection of potter's brushes

Printing techniques

with a thick root, trimmed obliquely and having a bent point was used for painting decorative leaf patterns. The so-called 'rose brush' was shorter, pointed at the top and thick at the root, and served for painting decorative rosebuds, stags, large leaves and other motifs. Brushes of the same thickness at the root and at the point were used for banding.

Potters in China and the Far East in general still make their own brushes. According to Bernard Leach, they use hair of various animals, including cat, badger, deer and dog. Only hair from certain places on the animal's body is selected where it is least abused by friction and the tips are not worn away, for example from the neck or the tail. The hairs are arranged in such a way as to allow use without trimming.

Figure 153 shows various commercially manufactured brushes used today. The best material available for brush making is marten, polecat and squirrel hair.

Printing is the youngest but commercially most widely used decoration technique. The category includes rubber stamping, die stamping, silk screen printing, lithographic and offset transfers.

However, the extent of this book allows only a description of those techniques which are most specific to ceramics. Detailed information on etching, engraving, lithographic and silk screen printing will be found in literature on graphic techniques. The procedure remains essentially the same, only ceramic colours are used instead of printing inks.

RUBBER STAMPING

The simplest printing technique is rubber stamping, which is used either under or over a fired glaze.

Every potter can make his rubber stamps by himself by cutting the outlines of a motif in hard rubber. For larger surfaces softer, more porous rubber is used (fig. 154). It is also possible to cut the ornament into a plaster or wooden block and mould it in clay or plaster. The mould thus produced is then cast in silicone rubber. A piece of rubber sponge should be glued between the stamp and the wooden handle to allow the stamping of curved surfaces (fig. 155). Unglazed bodies are stamped with printing or stamping ink. In the first case two parts normal underglaze colour are ground with one part printing varnish. If the mixture is too thick, it should be diluted with olive or clove oil (turpentine would make it too thin). The ground colour is rolled evenly on a glass plate

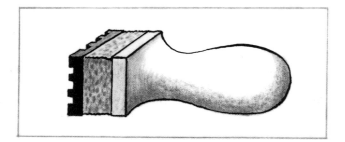

Fig. 154   Rubber stamp from porous rubber

Fig. 155   Stamping a curved surface using a rubber stamp

with a printer's rubber inking roller and the rubber stamp is pressed against it to take on colour. It is also possible to use commercial rubber stamping inks. For decoration of fired glazes two parts onglaze colour are ground with one part thick varnish prepared according to the recipe, or by use of a commercial product. A few drops of the colour prepared in this way are spread evenly on a gelatine stamping pad used to ink the rubber stamp.

The places which are to be decorated can be outlined beforehand with indelible pencil on the body or with China ink on the glaze. Both will burn in the fire, leaving no traces.

Once the stamped design has dried somewhat, but is still sticky, it is dusted with dry, finely ground ceramic colour. The best way is to use a wad of cotton wool. The colour will stick to the design and surplus dust is carefully blown off.

When biscuit is to be stamped prior to glazing, the areas adjacent to the design are sometimes difficult to clean. Also the rubber stamp often takes on body particles. In such cases the body is coated with a solution of soap, dextrin, gum arabic, etc., and stamped after the coat has dried. Needless to say, in such cases the body must be refired prior to glazing.

The stamp must be cleaned only with alcohol which does not attack rubber.

When precious metals, such as gold, silver or platinum, are to be used, about 15 parts of the metal solution are mixed with 1 part clove oil and spread evenly on a glass slab with a rubber spatula. If the mixture is too thin, it should be left in a warm place to acquire the desired consistency.

DIE STAMPING

The decoration to be printed is first etched or engraved in a steel, copper or zinc plate. A ceramic colour is carefully ground in the same way as for rubber stamping and, using a spatula, it is pressed into the etched or engraved pattern on the plate (fig. 156). The latter should be pre-heated. Excess colour is wiped off and the plate is polished.

The pattern is then transferred on to fine printing tissue paper which has been moistened with soapy water (fig. 157).

Fig. 156 Dressing a steel plate with printing ink

Fig. 157 Laying tissue printing paper on the plate

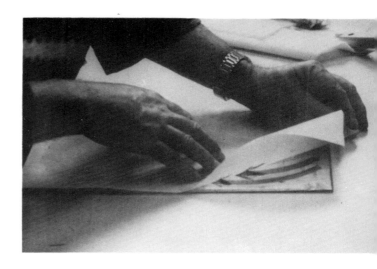

58
Dish
Creil, France, 1810
Stoneware with Ranston landscape printed in black
24 × 24 cm
Museum of Decorative Arts, Prague

The paper bearing the transferred design is then laid on the body and smoothed with a wet sponge and rolled with a leather or felt roller. The colour is transferred on to the body but the paper can be easily peeled off due to the effect of soap water.

Should the imprint be too weak, it is possible to improve it by dusting it with colour in the same way as for rubber stamping described above.

TRANSFERS

Multicoloured transfers are used mostly on fired glazes. The design is printed on paper with ceramic on-glaze colours, using the lithographic or offset printing process. Prior to use, however, the transfer (known also as the **decal**) must be given a coat of positive or negative lacquer. Cut transfers are then placed in clean water for about one minute and then laid on to a wetted polyurethane mat where they can remain for some time.

Transfers with negative lacquer are placed on the body with the paper facing up, pressed with a sponge and then the paper is carefully peeled off.

Positive transfers are placed on the body with the paper backing down (that is, against the body) and the decoration is carefully slid on to the pot.

In both cases the transfer must be smoothed with a natural sponge and a rubber doctor knife or squeegee to force out all water and air.

If the transfers are too old and therefore too dry, they are best moistened in lukewarm water, or a commercial colour and lacquer softener may be added to facilitate perfect adhesion of the transfer to the body and ensure unrippled surfaces. When thoroughly dry, the body should be washed with a sponge and warm water to remove remnants of the isolation coat. This is especially important if negative transfers are used.

59
Gentleman with Rose in Lapel
Pravoslav Rada, Czechoslovakia, 1983
Porcelain, photographic collage, silk screen printed on fired glaze; black, flower red and green; oil fired at 1340 °C, decoration at 800 °C
Diameter 30 cm
Private collection

Etching

SILK SCREEN PRINTING

Silk screen printing, or serigraphy, is a very old method of transferring decoration and lettering. Long before Christ, Chinese and Japanese potters used templates made from screens woven from women's hair, with delicate paper cutouts glued on both sides. Following World War II the silk screen printing technique, patented in Europe in the 19th century, became widely used in the ceramic industry.

The technique consists of transferring a decoration by means of a silk screen, a fine cloth stretched in a frame and made impervious in the places which are not to be printed. Through the open areas of mesh, colour, possibly also asphalt, is pressed onto the body using a spatula. The design can be either printed directly or on to a transfer paper.

The frames used in serigraphy are either wooden or metal. For studio use, wooden frames are quite sufficient but metal frames are better for large-scale operations. The mesh used for the application of colour is fine fabric, woven either from natural silk or from some manmade fibre such as nylon. Phosphor bronze or stainless steel wire mesh is used for slips, asphalt varnish used for etching, wax resist and other materials. Stencils used in ceramic silk screen printing are the same as those used in the printing industry. Information on their preparation will be found in the relevant literature.

The colours used in serigraphy are essentially ceramic colours. For printing purposes, they are mixed with commercial silk screen printing oil. It is also possible to use ready-made ceramic silk screen printing colours.

Apart from colours, other materials like slips, glazes, isolation pastes for etching and transfer varnishes may also be used. These materials must first be mixed with a suitable oil- or water-based bonding agent. For experimental work, other nontraditional materials like soft soap, paraffin oil, wax emulsion or vaseline can be used, often with surprising effects. However, this type of decoration is usually used only once and approaches monotype in character.

Genuine etching is a very difficult technique and its use is usually reserved for luxury porcelain wares. The glaze is etched to a depth of about one-tenth of a millimetre and gilded twice with dull gold, then burnished on the nonetched surfaces. The etching pattern is transferred on to the body by various methods.

In **hand etching** the pattern is engraved into a coat of asphalt covering the places to be etched, while the rest of the surface is protected by some wax resist. Etching is done with hydrofluoric acid.

When the pattern has been etched, the acid is washed off, the wax resist coat is removed by dipping the article in hot water and the asphalt is washed off with turpentine or kerosene. The wax which solidifies in water can be reused.

It is also possible to draw the pattern on to the body using a brush or a pen and asphalt varnish thinned with turpentine. The places which are to be etched are left bare.

In **dust etching**, a rubber or die stamp is first used to transfer the pattern on to the glaze and then dusted with fine asphalt dust. Prior to etching the body must be heated in a drying kiln to about 80 °C at which the asphalt grains melt, forming a smooth surface coat.

Another method involves the use of an **isolation paste**. The pattern is transferred from a steel plate on to the body in the usual manner but the printing colour is replaced by isolation paste. The transfer paper bearing the design is pressed against the body with a roller and left in place for 24 hours, then it is wetted with water containing some vinegar and carefully peeled off. If necessary, the pattern may be melted in the same way as in dust etching, and retouched with asphalt varnish (fig. 160).

Other transferring methods used in etching of ceramics include **silk screen transfers** (decals), **thermoplastic silk screen printing** and various **etching pastes**. These methods have been developed by various companies manufacturing and marketing ceramic chemicals (figs 158, 159 and 161).

IMITATION ETCHING

This cheap technique closely resembles genuine etching, which is quite expensive. Basically, it is printing a bright gold decoration on a base of matt colour. Imitation etching produces just the opposite effect from genuine etching, that is, the matt and glossy surfaces are reversed. Application methods include rubber stamping, dusting, serigraphy, transfers and spraying. The wares are fired twice, first the colour at about 800 °C, then

Photographic decoration

the gold decoration at about 700 °C. Some companies manufacture substances that require only single firing.

Essentially, the process enables transferring ceramic colours and pigments by means of a photographic emulsion. The first attempts at using photographic methods for this purpose date very far back. In fact, Josiah Wedgwood's youngest son, Thomas, is reputed to have experimented with the camera obscura, trying to use silver for transferring decoration on to pottery.

Photographs can be transferred in three ways. Using the indirect method, the image is developed on a light-sensitive gelatine emulsion applied to

Fig. 158   Laying tissue printing paper into a silk screen thermoplastic printing machine

Fig. 159   Printing with heated asphalt coat

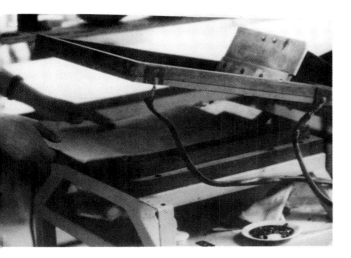

Fig. 160   Finished asphalt coat print

Fig. 161   Transferring decoration from printing paper to porcelain

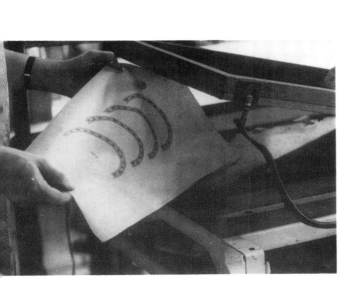

a glass plate. The emulsion is lifted and transferred on to the body and then dried and fired. In the direct method, the light-sensitive emulsion is applied directly on to the body, the image is exposed and the body is fired. There is also a third method which consists of transferring the image on to a transfer paper by means of silk screen or offset printing and the printed transfer is then used in the usual way.

The indirect method:

A glass plate is degreased and cleaned. The edges are bordered by thin strips of wax or plasticine and the plate is laid perfectly level. A few drops of glycerine are smeared on to the plate and a light-sensitive emulsion is then poured on. Pouring must be done in a darkroom using an orange light. After the emulsion has dried, a photographic slide is placed on to it and exposed in sunlight or using a fluorescent lamp. The ambient temperature must not exceed 45 °C. The exposure time must be trial-tested beforehand.

The exposed plate is then cooled in a room with a humid atmosphere. The hydroscopic emulsion not hardened by light absorbs moisture from the air, becoming sticky. If the environment is too dry, the emulsion may be moistened by breathing on it. The plate is then dusted with finely ground ceramic colour which will adhere to the sticky surface (after retouching the image, using a two per cent apothecary collodion solution). The dried collodion layer is carefully cut from the glass backing on three sides and immersed in a lukewarm solution of 25 g borax and 10 g sodium hydroxide dissolved in 1 litre of distilled water. When the collodion layer becomes unstuck, it is washed in clean lukewarm water to wash off the last residues of dichromate. The fourth side is now cut off from the glass and the whole collodion film is laid on to the body. The whole operation must be performed with the items submerged under water. When the pot is dry, it is fired at the correct firing temperature for the colour used.

The direct method is much more complicated and it is advisable to use well-tested ready-made substances marketed by manufacturers of photographic chemicals (Kodak, Picceramic, Rockland, etc.), strictly observing the instructions for use. Transferring images by silk screen or transfer printing is the same as that described on page 168.

DECORATION BY LASER

Industrial decoration of ceramic wares by laser technology is now tested by various manufacturers. The laser beam heats the substance used for decoration up to its evaporation point. Laser technology can be applied to many of the techniques discussed above.

Cutting and piercing of raw and biscuit bodies has been successfully tested under industrial conditions. The laser beam can also be used to thin the body to produce translucent patterns like lithophane, to produce traces in slip, under-glaze and on-glaze colour, for engraving or for relief decoration as in genuine etching.

One great advantage of decorating ceramics by laser is that no moulds or stencils are required. The entire process is automatically controlled by a computer using a simple drawing as a master. Programs can be changed within minutes.

Fig. 162 shows laser-produced decoration in fired on-glaze colour on a porcelain body.

Fig. 162   Decoration produced by laser

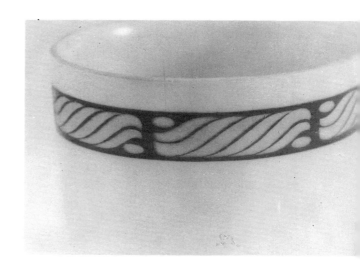

Recipes

RESISTS

Flour	8	Mix well into paste and apply to body. Spray over with underglaze colour with some dextrin added. Leave to dry and blow off resist with a stream of air. For softer biscuits use more kaolin and less flour, for hard biscuits the reverse. Without additional biscuit firing.
Kaolin	7	
Alcohol	5	

Beeswax	4	Dissolve wax in heated turpentine and ink. Apply mixture to body, let dry and spray with colour. Fire after drying.
Printer's ink	3	
Turpentine	5	

Beeswax	3	Applied in hot state on slip or unfired glaze. Will burn out in firing.
Paraffin oil	1	

Gum arabic	—	Using thick solution, draw on fired glaze. When dry, spray with on-glaze colour. When the colour is dry, wash gum off with water.

PRINTING VARNISHES

Linseed oil	5	Mix in a water bath (30 °C) and pour into green bottle. Place in sun. Leave bottle unstopped but use a cloth to protect from dust. Add green vitriol and shake to obtain an almost colourless varnish. Varnish for underglaze printing (after Hegemann).
Walnut oil	2	
Venetian balsam	3	

Linseed oil	400	Mix and boil until cooled drop forms thread. Then add 20 parts tar by weight and strain. Sticky varnish for on-glaze printing (after Hegemann).
Rapeseed oil	100	
Colophony	12.5	
Wood tar	6.5	
Red lead	6.5	

PROTECTIVE COATS FOR PLATES

Asphalt	18	Dissolve asphalt in hot turpentine. Add remaining ingredients while stirring continuously. Beware, highly inflammable! Protective varnish.
Turpentine	48	
Beeswax	12.5	
Burgundy resin	10	
Thick varnish	5	
Beef suet	1	

Asphalt	20	Dissolve asphalt in hot turpentine and add stearin and beeswax while stirring. Protective varnish for steel plates.
Turpentine	20	
Stearin	24	
Beeswax	7	

Burgundy resin	9	Dissolve on medium heat, pour into water and knead well. Prior to use heat somewhat and stick to plate edge. Wax for plate bordering before etching.
Beeswax	5	
Beef suet	3	

ETCHING SOLUTIONS

Water	420	Dissolve chloride and tartaric acid in water and mix with nitric acid. Beware, mercury chloride is very toxic! For etching steel plates.
Mercury chloride	15	
Tartaric acid	1	
Nitric acid	16-20 drops	

Water	5	Dissolve mercury in nitric acid and mix with water and alcohol. For etching steel plates.
Alcohol	1	
Nitric acid	1	
Mercury	1-2	

Water	1	Mix together.
Nitric acid	1	For etching steel plates.

Wine alcohol 80%	12	Mix alcohol and acid with silver nitrate dissolved in a small quantity of water For etching steel plates.
Nitric acid	8	
Silver nitrate	1	

Iodine	2	Dissolve iodide in water and then add iodine. For etching steel plates.
Potassium iodide	2	
Water	100	

Ferric chloride	1	Dissolve and filter through cotton wool. Keep in dark place. When solution turns green due to large copper content, etching capacity is at its end. For etching copper and brass plates.
Water	4	

Nitric acid	1	Dissolve gum arabic in water and mix with acid. For surface etching of zinc plates.
Gum arabic	10	
Water	100	

Nitric acid	15	Mix together. For deep etching of zinc plates.
Hydrochloric acid	10	
Water	100	

SOAP SOLUTION FOR DRESSING PRINTING PAPERS

Grain soap	10 g	Dissolve and leave to evaporate by one-third. Dress paper using brush and place on plate with dressed side down. Used to dress printing tissue paper.
Soda crystals	10 g	
Water	100 ccm	

PROTECTIVE VARNISH FOR PORCELAIN ETCHING

Wax	3	Dissolve all solids in heated turpentine. Protective varnish A, for engraving with steel burins. If further diluted with turpentine, used for painting and drawing.
Stearin	2	
Asphalt	30	
Suet	1	
Turpentine	40-50	

Asphalt	25	Dissolve ingredients one by one in benzol. Protective varnish B.
Colophony	10	
Beeswax	5	
Dammar resin	10	
Vaseline	2	
Venetian balsam	2	
Benzol	60	

Asphalt	50	Dissolve all ingredients in heated turpentine. Protective asphalt coat for places which are not to be etched.
Stearin	15	
Beeswax	30	
Turpentine	200	

ETCHING SOLUTION FOR PORCELAIN

Concentrated hydrofluoric acid	6	Mix together. For deep etching.
Water	3	
Sulphuric acid	1	

ETCHING PASTE FOR RUBBER STAMPING

Ammonium fluoride	20	Dissolve ammonium fluoride, salt and soda in hydrofluoric acid using a rubber or lead vessel. Add sulphuric acid and potassium fluoride dissolved in hydrochloric acid. Add enough water glass to make the mixture spread well on a felt rubber stamping pad. Apply etching paste with rubber stamp, leave for 24 hours and wash off.
Kitchen salt	3	
Soda	3	
Concentrated hydrofluoric acid	8	
Concentrated sulphuric acid	4	
Potassium fluoride	1	
Hydrochloric acid	2	
Water glass	as needed	

DRYING

PHOTOSENSITIVE EMULSIONS
(after Puskov)

Distilled water	100 ml	Mix all ingredients together and when completely dissolved, apply to a glass plate.
Ammonia	5 ml	
Whipped and rested egg white	20 ml	
Fish glue	20 ml	
Glucose	40 g	
Ammonium dichromate	2 g	

Distilled water	100 ml	Proceed as above.
Sugar	5 g	
Ammonium dichromate	2 g	
Glycerine	2-8 drops	

Distilled water	100 ml	Proceed as above.
Whipped and rested egg-white	20 ml	
Honey	15 ml	
Ammonium dichromate	2 g	

Water	1000 ml	Bath used for cleaning of glass plates.
Hydrochloric acid	100 ml	
Potassium dichromate	10 g	

Water	1000 ml	Bath for removal of collodion remnants from glass plates.
Borax	25 g	
Sodium hydroxide	10 g	

Distilled water	100 ml	The solution is filtered through gauze and applied on a paper backing and is left to dry. After exposure, the sensitive film is moistened with steam and dusted with finely ground ceramic colour. Coat body with a 3% solution of spruce resin in ether. Glue the image on to body, moisten paper backing with warm water and peel off carefully. Dried body is fired.
Ferric ammonium citrate	20 g	
Ferric chloride	5 g	
Sugar	5 g	
Wheat starch	7-10 g	

Prior to firing, water must be removed from ceramic wares, which is sometimes quite difficult and an incorrect procedure may result in great waste during drying and firing.

The water contained in the ceramic wares is of three types:

(a) mechanically retained (free) water which fills the cavities in the mass of the material and the spaces between the particles. Such water retains the character of a fluid and its evaporation causes the greatest shrinkage;

(b) physico-chemically bound (combined) water forming a film on the particle surface and differing in character from free water. However, it can be removed by prolonged drying;

(c) chemically bound water (crystalline) which is retained in the crystalline structure of the batch and will not be removed by drying but only by firing (at about 500 °C).

The rapidity of drying depends then not only on the surface water evaporation rate but also on how water from the inside of the body wall can permeate to the surface.

Drying will be easiest with wares made from materials of low plasticity containing fireclay or other grog. Since such materials have a low shrinkage, there are enough pores between the particles to permit release of water during drying and firing of the bodies.

Fine-grained and highly plastic materials are not so easy to dry, since they develop a greater shrinkage and the capillary action of water from inside of the body, especially a thick-walled one, takes longer. It is therefore vital to make sure that the pores are not closed during drying, otherwise the body could shatter or shiver. Whenever possible, it is advisable to pierce the body on the reverse side (see the chapter on modelling).

A well-tested and simple method of slowing down the evaporation rate is to cover the body with paper, or to let it dry slowly in a room with high relative humidity.

To prevent deformation, cracking or shattering of the body, care must be taken that the body dries evenly on all sides. Never place a drying pot against a wall, but always leave it standing free, with enough space all around.

Some complicated parts, protruding parts of figurines, thin pot rims, etc., must sometimes be covered with a wet cloth to achieve uniform drying of the whole article.

Another danger experienced during drying and firing is caused by a resistance that rough-sur-

KILNS AND FIRING

faced supports or kiln furniture offer to the smooth and shrinking pot bottom or figure base. A reliable solution is to place fine work on tissue paper and large wares on newsprint because, as the body shrinks, the paper travels with it, preventing possible deformations.

Especially suitable for studio work are electric infrared heaters. If located correctly, they can produce a uniform drying rate.

Each firing, with which the potter's work culminates, is a festive moment and those who have never experienced it cannot know the suspense with which the potter opens the cooled kiln. Naturally, today's easy-to-operate electric kilns have reduced the risk of failure to an absolute minimum, but equally their introduction has robbed the artist of the joy of mastering the unpredictable live fire. Simple operation and availability of low-temperature electric kilns on the one hand, and the hard work involved and nonavailability of open fire kilns of high temperatures on the other, explain why most ceramic artists today choose to work with softer clays.

If we follow the evolution of kiln design and compare ancient Grecian, Roman or Oriental kilns with some of their modern counterparts, we cannot fail to notice the striking similarity which no modern development can obscure. The only essential modern change has been the introduction of new fuels such as oil, gas or electricity and of the continuous tunnel kiln brought about by the needs of large-scale mechanized production.

Roughly speaking, kilns are usually classified according to the direction of the fire draught.

60
Kiln model
China, Han dynasty,
1st century AD
Pottery with iridescent
lead glaze
14 × 18 × 25 cm
National Gallery, Prague

174

XXXII
Large plate
Ursula Scheid, West Germany, 1983
Stoneware, gas fired at 1360 °C
40 × 37.5 cm
Private collection

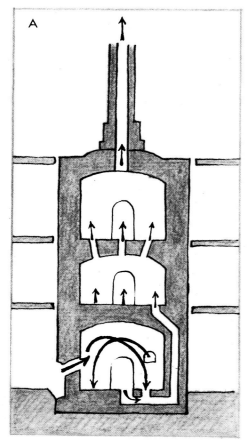

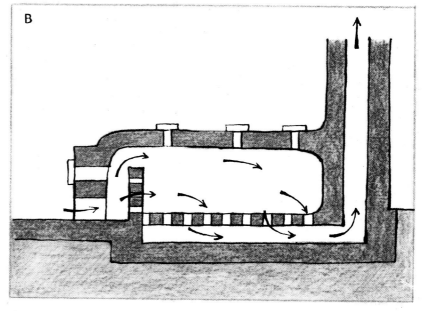

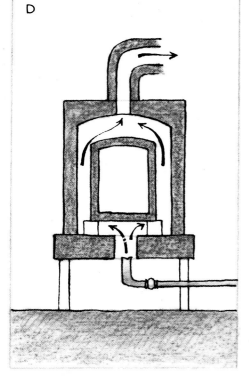

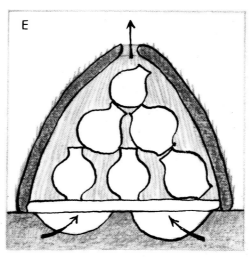

Fig. 163 Schematic diagrams of some kilns:
(A) Multiple-storey porcelain kiln; the bottom (down-draught) chamber is used to fire glaze; the first storey is used for biscuit firing and the top storey for preheating saggars
(B) Cassel kiln with partition wall
(C) Oriental kiln
(D) Gas-fired muffle kiln
(E) Primitive field kiln

Kiln types

UP-DRAUGHT KILNS

The furnace is located under a grate bottom, through which fire enters the kiln proper, passes between the stacked wares and leaves through the flue and the chimney. In fact, primitive field kilns were based on the same principle (fig. 163E). These kilns were built from clay and wickerwork for a single pot or a number of pots. Around the pot or pots enough wood was packed for the firing. Holes provided at the bottom induced air and smoke to pass out through the upper outlet. After firing, the top of the kiln had to be demolished to take out the fired pot.

DOWN-DRAUGHT KILNS

The fire rises from the furnace to the roof, returns to the floor and then leaves through the chimney or, in the case of a multiple-storey kiln, enters the next chamber (see fig. 163A).

HORIZONTAL DRAUGHT KILNS

Horizontal draught kilns, termed also Cassel kilns, have the hearth located on the front, shorter side of the kiln, and are separated from the chamber by a partition which prevents ashes and other impurities from entering the chamber and controls an even distribution of fire through the hearth. The flames pass horizontally between the stacked wares and utlimately reach the chimney (fig. 163B). A transition type between up-draught and horizontal draught kilns are Oriental kilns, shown in fig. 163C.

MUFFLE KILNS

In muffle kilns the wares do not come in contact with fire, because they are loaded in an inside chamber known as a muffle which is heated by fire on all sides. Fig. 163D shows a schematic diagram of a gas-fired muffle kiln.

ELECTRIC AND GAS FIRED KILNS

These kilns utilizing modern quality fuels are most suitable for studio work because they do not require a bulky and expensive chimney. Likewise their operation is quite simple and comfortable. Fig. 164 shows an electrically fired box kiln with a volume of one cubic metre.

Packing a kiln

When fired, standard pottery wares are usually exposed to the fire and smoke. Pots are usually boxed in the kiln, that is, two pots of the same size are placed on top of each other rim to rim, naturally unglazed.

Open fire is still used for firing unglazed fireclay architectural or garden ceramics, because the flame and smoke give these wares the required characteristic patina.

However, fine wares must be protected from dirt as well as undesirable reduction and are, therefore, fired in muffle kilns or in saggars placed in regular kilns. In muffles, wares are packed using fireclay shelves and supports (figs 165-167). Some types of fireclay furniture used to prevent the melted glaze from bonding the pot to a shelf or floor are shown in fig. 166.

(a) **Stilts:** the ware is supported by the points or by the upper edges of the arms. Stilts are also used for firing decorated porcelain, to separate plates and dishes.

(b) **Saddles:** these triangular bars are used to support oval and elongated dishes and bowls.

(c) **Crank:** this type of furniture is luted to the pot bottom using a mixture of aluminium hydroxide or alumina and dextrin. The pot with an attached support is easily placed even deep inside the oven where handling wares with unattached supports would be extremely difficult. This method is used to advantage by some large manufacturers who have several standardized bottom sizes with corresponding supports.

(d) **Pips:** these small supports are used for wares glazed on the underside. After firing, the rough spots produced by the pips are ground off.

◄

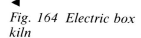

Fig. 164   Electric box kiln

◄

Fig. 165   Kiln car stacked with wares

Fig. 166   Some types of kiln fireclay furniture

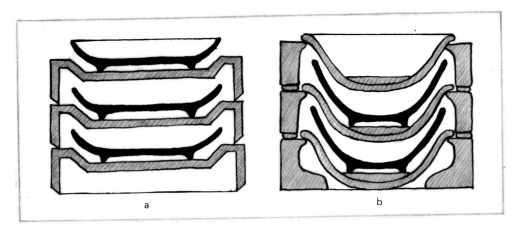

Fig. 167 Saggars
(a) for dishes
(b) for bowls

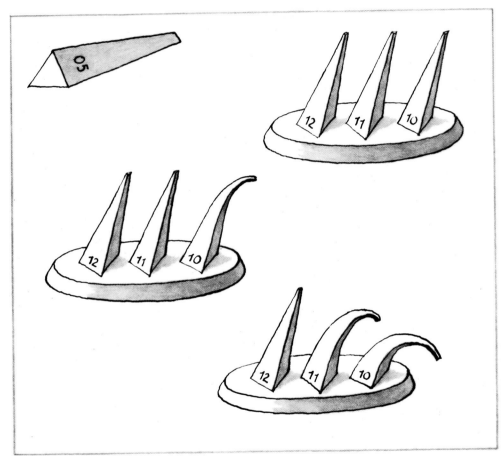

Fig. 168 Seger cones
(see opposite)

(e) **Spurs:** these supports enable bunging (that is, stacking) of several dishes or plates.

Sticking of wares with melted glaze can also be prevented by **bat wash**, a mixture of calcinated alumina and a bit of clay and water. It is brushed on the saggars and props. A thin dust of alumina or some refractory material is also sufficient.

To prevent contamination of the fired ware with fireclay dust, saggar and prop bottoms and muffle roofs are washed with **kiln wash**, usually a soft glaze.

Pottery, porous and stoneware articles usually require no special protection but porcelain, whose body becomes pyroplastic during firing, must often be propped by various props to prevent deformation. The support must be of the same material as the body to have the same shrinkage. To prevent warping, bowls, dishes and other wares of this type are sometimes fired with the lids on. Prior to glazing they must be isolated with a mixture of stearin and alumina. Cups are likewise fired boxed and luted with a mixture of dextrin and aluminium hydroxide.

Firing

Measuring the temperature

The temperature and method of firing of individual wares differ and have already been discussed earlier. What remains to be dealt with is reduction firing of porcelain which is used to obtain whiteness. The reason is that a reducing atmosphere changes ferric yellow-firing compounds into ferrous ones which fire white. The procedure is to start with an oxidizing firing up to 1030 °C, then reduction firing is maintained up to 1250 °C when the glaze begins to melt. From this moment until the end a neutral atmosphere is maintained in the kiln. During reduction firing the temperature must not be allowed to drop, because this, followed by a temperature rise, would result in boiling of the glaze and air bubbles produced by gas.

Reduction firing is also required by some coloured glazes and lustres. In open fire furnaces a reducing atmosphere is produced simply by closing the air inlet, which results in imperfect combustion. Reduction also depends on the type of fuel used. For example, Bernard Leach writes that some woods (such as common elder, oak, elm and ashtree) produce a greater reduction than, for example, horse chestnut, appletree or walnut, which are better for oxidizing fire. Even the appearance of the flames may be misleading. For instance, both spruce and pine develop much smoke, yet the atmosphere in the kiln is more of an oxidizing type.

In electric and muffle kilns reduction is achieved by throwing inside some substance producing a lot of carbon. However, most of these substances harm the heating elements. According to element manufacturers, the least dangerous material is charcoal.

The firing temperature in the kiln is checked by pyrometric cones, by pyrometers of various designs, but also by estimation; an experienced potter is able to tell the temperature by the colour of the fire or the gloss of the glaze which is observed when a chip of wood or a wad of paper is thrown inside the kiln.

Some manufacturers check the firing of their wares on the basis of specimens removed during the firing process.

One of the most widely used methods involves pyrometric cones made of ceramic materials and calibrated for deformation at a certain temperature. When the tip of the cone bends towards the base, the calibrated temperature has been achieved. It is very important to set the cones properly, as incorrect positioning would distort the readings. A correctly positioned cone should tilt some 6° to 10° away from the perpendicular.

Cones are calibrated with numbers corresponding to a certain temperature. The table over leaf shows numbers of Seger cones used in Europe as well as American Orton and British Staffordshire cones (but see also *Note* below). Listings relate to 'large' cones used in the industry. Small cones which are used rather for small laboratory kilns have different designations.

There is also a table showing cone numbers and corresponding temperatures given both in degrees Celsius and Fahrenheit.

Note:
The producers of the pyrometric cones have recently adopted a new marking system directly reflecting temperature: E.g. cone No. 8 = 1250 °C is now marked No. 125, cone No. 9 = 1280 °C is now marked No. 128, etc.

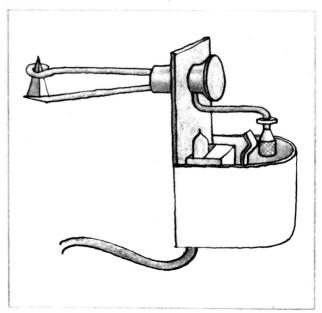

Fig. 169 A device which will automatically switch off an electric kiln when a pyrometric cone deforms

PYROMETRIC CONES

CONE NUMBER	BRITISH STAFFORDSHIRE °C	EUROPEAN SEGER °C	AMERICAN ORTON °C	Colour of heat	Fired product
022	600	600	585		
022A	625	—	—		Bright gold;
021	650	650	602	Initial red	soft Oriental enamels;
020	670	670	625		raku glazes
019	690	690	668		
018	710	710	696		
017	730	730	727		
016	750	750	767		
015	790	—	790	Dark red	
015A	—	790	—		
014	815	—	834		
014A	—	815	—		
013	835	—	869		On-glaze colours;
013A	—	835	—		enamels; lustres;
012	855	—	866	Red to	soft glazes; porcelain
012A	—	855	—	cherry red	and stoneware biscuit
011	880	—	886		
011A	—	880	—		
010	900	—	887		
010A	—	900	—		
09	920	—	915		
09A	—	920	—		
08	940	—	945		
08A	950	940	—		
07	960	—	973		
07A	970	960	—	Cherry	
06	980	—	991		
06A	990	980	—		
05	1000	—	1031		Pottery; tiles; maiolica;
05A	1010	1000	—		soft porous ware
04	1020	—	1050		
04A	1030	1020	—		
03	1040	—	1086		
03A	1050	1040	—	Light cherry	
02	1060	—	1101		
02A	1070	1060	—		
01	1080	—	1117		
01A	1090	1080	—		
1	1100	—	1136		
1A	1110	1100	—		
2	1120	—	1142		
2A	1130	1120	—		
3	1140	—	1152	Orange to light orange	
3A	1150	1140	—		
4	1160	—	1168		
4A	1170	1160	—		
5	1180	—	1177		
5A	1190	1180	—		Hard porous ware;
6	1200	—	1201		fritted porcelain;
6A	1215	1200	—		bone china; stoneware;
7	1230	1230	1215		soft Oriental porcelain
7A	1240	—	—		
8	1250	1250	1236	Yellow-white	
8A	1260	—	—		
8B	1270	—	—		
9	1280	1280	1260		
9A	1290	—	—		
10	1300	1300	1285		
10A	1310	—	—	White	
11	1320	1320	1294		
12	1350	1350	1306		
13	1380	1380	1321		
14	1410	1410	1388	Intense white	
15	1435	1435	1424		
16	1460	1460	1455		Hard porcelain;
17	1480	1480	1477		fireclay products
18	1500	1500	1500	Dazzling	
19	1520	1520	1520	white heat	
20	1530	1530	1542		

TEMPERATURE CONVERSION TABLE

If the figure in the central column is in °C, the corresponding temperature in °F will be found in the right-hand column.
If the figure in the central column is in °F, the corresponding temperature in °C will be found in the left-hand column.

°C		°F	°C		°F	°C		°F
−18	0	32	354	670	1238	727	1340	2444
−12	10	50	360	680	1256	732	1350	2462
−7	20	68	366	690	1274	738	1360	2480
−1	30	86	371	700	1292	743	1370	2498
4	40	104	377	710	1310	749	1380	2516
10	50	122	382	720	1328	754	1390	2534
16	60	140	388	730	1346	760	1400	2552
21	70	158	393	740	1364	766	1410	2570
27	80	176	399	750	1382	771	1420	2588
32	90	194	404	760	1400	777	1430	2606
38	100	212	410	770	1418	782	1440	2624
43	110	230	416	780	1436	788	1450	2642
49	120	248	421	790	1454	793	1460	2660
54	130	266	427	800	1472	799	1470	2678
60	140	284	432	810	1490	804	1480	2696
66	150	302	438	820	1508	810	1490	2714
71	160	320	443	830	1526	816	1500	2732
77	170	338	449	840	1544	821	1510	2750
82	180	356	454	850	1562	827	1520	2768
88	190	374	460	860	1580	832	1530	2786
93	200	392	466	870	1598	838	1540	2804
99	210	410	471	880	1616	843	1550	2822
104	220	428	477	890	1634	849	1560	2840
110	230	446	482	900	1652	854	1570	2858
116	240	464	488	910	1670	860	1580	2876
121	250	482	493	920	1688	866	1590	2894
127	260	500	499	930	1706	871	1600	2912
132	270	518	504	940	1724	877	1610	2930
138	280	536	510	950	1742	882	1620	2948
143	290	554	516	960	1760	888	1630	2966
149	300	572	521	970	1778	893	1640	2984
154	310	590	527	980	1796	899	1650	3002
160	320	608	532	990	1814	904	1660	3020
166	330	626	538	1000	1832	910	1670	3038
171	340	644	543	1010	1850	916	1680	3056
177	350	662	549	1020	1868	921	1690	3074
182	360	680	554	1030	1886	927	1700	3092
188	370	698	560	1040	1904	932	1710	3110
193	380	716	566	1050	1922	938	1720	3128
199	390	734	571	1060	1940	943	1730	3146
204	400	752	577	1070	1958	949	1740	3164
210	410	770	582	1080	1976	954	1750	3182
216	420	788	588	1090	1994	960	1760	3200
221	430	806	593	1100	2012	966	1770	3218
227	440	824	599	1110	2030	971	1780	3236
232	450	842	604	1120	2048	977	1790	3254
238	460	860	610	1130	2066	982	1800	3272
243	470	878	616	1140	2084	988	1810	3290
249	480	896	621	1150	2102	993	1820	3308
254	490	914	627	1160	2120	999	1830	3326
260	500	932	632	1170	2138	1004	1840	3344
266	510	950	638	1180	2156	1010	1850	3362
271	520	968	643	1190	2174	1016	1860	3380
277	530	986	649	1200	2192	1021	1870	3398
282	540	1004	654	1210	2210	1027	1880	3416
288	550	1022	660	1220	2228	1032	1890	3434
293	560	1040	666	1230	2246	1038	1900	3452
299	570	1058	671	1240	2264	1043	1910	3470
304	580	1076	677	1250	2282	1049	1920	3488
310	590	1094	682	1260	2300	1054	1930	3506
316	600	1112	688	1270	2318	1060	1940	3524
321	610	1130	693	1280	2336	1066	1950	3542
327	620	1148	699	1290	2354	1071	1960	3560
332	630	1166	704	1300	2372	1077	1970	3578
338	640	1184	710	1310	2390	1082	1980	3596
343	650	1202	716	1320	2408	1088	1990	3614
349	660	1220	721	1330	2426	1093	2000	3632

To convert °C to °F: temp. °C × 1.8 + 32 = temp. °F
°F to °C: (temp. °F − 32) 0.555 = temp. °C

Recipes

Cones are placed against the kiln spyhole and must be closely observed. As the temperature rises, the tip of the cone starts bending. When the tip touches the prop, the correct temperature has been reached. To be sure, usually three cones are placed inside the kiln in sequential numbers, of which the middle one corresponds to the desired temperature (see fig. 168).

Pyrometers are much more precise, however. The most widely used type is the thermoelectric (de Chatelier) pyrometer.

In principle, the pyrometer is a thermoelectric couple composed of two wires of different metals. When heated, electric current is generated in the weld of the two wires. The current is measured by a millivoltmeter calibrated directly in °C. The wires are insulated from each other by ceramic tubes and placed inside a refractory sheath. For temperatures to about 1000 °C alumel-chromel thermocouples are used, while pyrometers for temperatures up to 1300 °C use a platinum wire coupled with another made of an alloy of platinum and rhodium. To compensate for distortion of the measured values, the pyrometric tube and the meter must be connected by compensation leads. In electric kilns pyrometric sensors are directly coupled to the controls and when the desired temperature has been achieved, they automatically switch off. The accuracy of these pyrometers is usually ± 5 °C.

The most recent development in temperature measuring is digital meters which are fully automated and programmable.

American manufacturers sometimes use a special switching device in their electric kilns. It is a pyrometric cone carried between two arms. When the cone bends at an appropriate temperature, the arms close a contact and the kiln is switched off (fig. 169).

The ceramic industry successfully uses optical and radiation pyrometers. In optical (spectral) pyrometers the colour of a heated resistance filament is compared with the colour in the kiln. In radiation pyrometers the thermal radiation from the kiln interior is transmitted to a sensor via a system of reflectors. The electric voltage thus generated is measured with a galvanometer calibrated in °C.

Alumina	1	Mix with water to
Kaolin	1	make thin slurry. Protective kiln wash.
Silica sand	6	Mix with water to
Kaolin	4	make thick slurry. Isolation bat wash.
Aluminium		Mix with water to
hydroxide	2	make thick slurry.
Alumina	3	Isolation bat wash.
Kaolin	5	
Aluminium		Mix with water to
hydroxide	10	make thick slurry.
Dextrin	80	For luting kiln furni-
Glycerine	3	ture and boxed cups.
Paraffin	8	Melt and mix.
Aluminium		Mixture for isolating
hydroxide	2	lids fired on pots.
Powdered clay	1	Mix powdered
Powdered fireclay	1	ingredients with water
Baryte (heavy spar)	1	to make thick paste.
Water glass as needed		Kiln lining cement. Unsuitable for electric kilns. Use immediately.
Powdered clay	2	Mix with water to
Powdered fireclay	2	make paste.
Lead oxide	1	Cement for ceramic kiln linings.
Powdered clay	1	Mix with water to
Fine silica sand	1	make paste.
Powdered borax	1	Cement for ceramic kiln linings.
Refractory clay	13	Mix with water to
Feldspar	6	make paste. Lead
Lead oxide as needed		oxide added according to desired meltability. Saggar cement.
Kaolin	1	Grind to make thin,
Powdered refractory		smooth slurry.
clay	1	Saggar cement.
Water glass as needed		

RESTORING CERAMICS

Powdered fireclay	3	Grind to make thin slurry.
Red lead	1	
Water glass	as needed	Saggar cement. Use immediately.
Glaze	2	Mix with water to make thin slurry. For coating saggar insides.
Porcelain paste	1	
Fine fireclay	6	Grind with water to make thin slurry. For coating saggar insides.
Feldspar	5	

Damaged ceramic wares can rarely be restored in such a way that the damage is invisible. Restoration is largely limited to repairs performed in the cold state, that is, to cementing shards together or replacing minor missing parts. Only exceptionally is it possible to repair minor damage to the decoration or glaze with ceramic materials and refire the article.

Prior to cementing fragments together, the shards must be carefully cleaned along the fractured surfaces. Wares with open bodies are cleaned with alcohol or benzine, porcelain fragments may be boiled in water with the addition of two per cent sulphuric acid. Care should be taken not to damage the joints.

Prior to cementing, the fragments should be put together and grouped in several groups. It is advisable to cement the groups first and then assemble large pieces thus produced.

The fragments are cemented one by one, always after the preceding bond is firm. If the body is porous, the fractured surfaces should first be dressed with thinned cement to fill in the pores. The pieces are left to dry and only afterwards are cemented together in the usual way.

The cemented pieces must be supported or clamped together in a suitable manner whilst drying. Wooden or metal clamps and spring pegs may be used to advantage. Another good method is to place the mended article in a bed of sand to hold the joint level.

Any missing parts can be modelled right on the body with plastic wax or plaster mixed with glue and water. When the modelled piece is thoroughly dry, it is taken out carefully and bonded with a suitable cement. Missing decoration may be painted in tempera or oil paints and lacquered to give the article a glaze effect. When the glossy effect of oil paints is undesirable, it may be dulled with a matt tincture.

61
Ikebana vase in the form of a fireman's bucket
Sakata Tomiya, 13th master of the Hagi workshop,
Japan, 20th century
Stoneware, celadon glaze
Height 30.5 cm
National Gallery, Prague

Recipes

Decoration painted on a fired glaze and missing gold decoration may be repaired with ceramic colours and genuine gold and fired then in a muffle kiln.

According to Rathgen, faded, weathered coloured glazes are best restored by abrasion with fine moistened powdered pumice and soft cork. Gloss can be restored with poppyseed oil or, alternatively, paraffin.

However, the best method of restoring faded or scratched glazes is to refire the article in a glost-fire. Unfortunately, this is to be recommended only for pots one has made oneself or wares whose batch composition and method of manufacture are beyond doubt. Sgraffito and painting under transparent glazes can be refired with comparative safety. On the other hand, run or reduction glazes should not be restored in this way.

Biscuit wares are conserved with a thin, hot solution of gelatine with some formalin added. The body must be warmed and the work must be done in a warm environment to inhibit gelatinization. Other methods of conservation include impregnating the body with Dammar tincture or dipping it in hot paraffin, but this also has its disadvantages because as the body cools, a paraffin film is formed on the surface and is very difficult to remove. Porcelain biscuit need not be conserved, as it suffices to wash it with thick soap lather.

Naturally, if you are the maker of the article to be restored or conserved, you can afford to be more radical than if you work with wares made by somebody else or with antiquities. Should the latter be the case, it is advisable to consider carefully what method to use in order not to damage the item even further.

The modern chemical industry constantly develops new cements, bonding agents, lacquers and conservation agents which may be used to advantage when restoring ceramic wares, provided that instructions for use are strictly observed.

PLASTIC WAX

White wax	2	Melt wax and lard and
Yellow wax	4	mix with oxide. Knead
Pork lard	1	well when cold.
Ferric oxide	2	Used for modelling missing fragments.

Yellow wax	200	Melt wax and mix
Venetian balsam	25	with remaining
Pork lard	12	ingredients. Mix well
Armenian bole	110	and pour in cold water. Knead well. Used for modelling missing fragments.

DAMMAR TINCTURE

Dammar resin	3	Dissolve dammar in
Xylene	9	xylene, filter and mix
Bleached poppyseed oil	4	with solution of oil and turpentine.
Turpentine	30	Used for conserving biscuit fragments.

MATT TINCTURE FOR OIL PAINTS

Turpentine	200	Dissolve wax and
Mastic (asphalt cake)	1	mastic in turpentine.
White wax	4	Add lavender oil
Lavender oil	10	which will cloud the solution. When settled, the solution will be clear. To subdue gloss of oil paints used to repair decoration of old pottery.

CEMENTS AND BONDING AGENTS

Slaked lime	2	Mix lime and clay
Powdered fat clay	2	with eggwhite to make
Fresh eggwhite		thin slurry.
	as needed	For immediate use. Use cold.

Plaster	1	Grind plaster with oil
Olive oil	1	and add eggwhite.
Fresh eggwhite	4	For immediate use. Use cold.

Fresh eggwhite	5	Mix eggwhite with
Powdered burnt lime	2	lime and add water
Water	2	with plaster.
Plaster	11	For immediate use. Use cold.

| Casein | 1 | Mix. |
| Water glass | 6 | For immediate use. Use cold. |

| Casein | 4 | Mix lime in little water and mix with casein. For immediate use. Use cold. |
| Slaked lime | 1 | |

Glue	20	Dissolve glue in heated acetic acid and mix with ammonium dichromate. Keep in brown bottle. For immediate use. Use cold. Expose cemented article to sunlight for several hours.
Acetic acid 90%	30	
Powdered ammonium dichromate	1	

Alcohol	1	Boil together until thick. Heat lightly before use.
Vinegar	1	
Gelatine	1	

Venetian balsam	1	Melt together and mix well. Use hot.
White wax	2	
Colcothar	4	
Colophony	8	

| Shellac in alcohol | | Use concentrated solution. Use cold. |

Mastic	3	Dissolve mastic and shellac in turpentine heated in a water bath. Use cold.
Shellac	2	
Turpentine	1	

Burgundy resin	4	Melt resins and sulphur, mix with kaolin and make sticks. For bonding, heat both repaired article and stick.
Sulphur	6	
White shellac	1	
Mastic	2	
Elemi gum	2	
Powdered kaolin	5	

| Colophony | 5 | Melt colophony and add chalk, stirring continuously. Make sticks. Sticks can be coloured with argillaceous pigments. For bonding, heat both repaired article and stick. |
| Floated whiting | 6-7 | |

White shellac	18	Melt shellac and add balsam and zinc white, stirring continuously. Make sticks. For bonding, heat both repaired article and stick.
Venetian balsam	2	
Zinc white	1	

Plaster	4	Mix plaster with finely ground gum arabic and add borax solution to make thick paste. Slowly curing agent. Curing time 30 hours.
Gum arabic	1	
Concentrated solution of borax	as needed	

Powdered slaked lime	1	Mix together. For immediate use. Hardens quickly.
Plaster	5	
Fresh eggwhite	2	

Soft soap	5	Dissolve soap and borax in hot water, casein in cold water, and mix both until smooth. For bonding ceramics with fabrics.
Powdered borax	2	
Boiling water	30	
Powdered casein	15	
Cold water	40	

Natural rubber (caoutchouc)	5	Dissolve rubber and mastic in chloroform in a warm water bath. Inflammable! Use cold.
Mastic	1	
Chloroform (trichlormethane)	4	

White shellac	15	Dissolve shellac, mastic and balsam in alcohol in a warm water bath. Use cold.
Mastic	5	
Venetian balsam	1	
Alcohol	55	

Powdered slaked lime	25	Mix lime and alum and grind with blood until smooth. For immediate use. Use cold.
Powdered alum	3	
Bull's blood	20	

Zinc white	20	Mix zinc white and chalk just prior to use and grind well with water glass. For immediate use. Use cold.
Floated whiting	1	
Water glass	10	

62
Tile with St George
Bohemia, 15th century
Unglazed pottery, hand-pressed in a wooden mould
18 × 18 cm
Museum of Decorative Arts, Prague

MATHEMATICS OF CERAMIC DESIGN

BONDING AGENTS HARDENED IN FIRING

Finely ground fired clay	1	Clay of the same type as that used for the body is mixed with glass and water to make a thick paste. 5-10% zinc oxide is added as needed. For about 1250°.
Powdered glass	0.5-1	
Zinc oxide	as needed	

Porcelain glaze	6	Grind with water to make slurry. For porcelain firing temperatures.
Finely ground plain porcelain shards	10	
Floated whiting	1	

Powdered quartz	8	Grind with water to make slurry. For porcelain firing temperatures.
Powdered feldspar	5	
Powdered marble	85	
Powdered porcelain biscuit	85	

Ground porcelain potshards	2	Grind with water to make slurry. For muffle colour firing temperature.
Lead flux	1	

Red lead	9	Grind red lead, borax and quartz with water to make smooth paste. Add zinc oxide as needed. For muffle colour firing temperature.
Powdered borax	5	
Powdered quartz	3	
Zinc oxide	as needed	

Powdered quartz	2	Mix all ingredients and mix with turpentine to make paste. For muffle colour firing temperature.
Powdered borax	4	
White lead	12	
Zinc oxide	2	

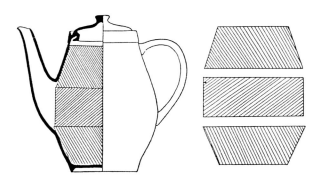

When designing various table and kitchen wares and other utility articles, the designer must calculate their capacity. This is done by dividing the article into as many geometrical bodies as possible and calculating their volumes whose sum then expresses the approximate capacity of the article.

An example shown on this page illustrates how to calculate the capacity of a jug using a sum of the volumes of a cylinder and two truncated cones. Naturally, if the article is divided into more bodies, the calculation will be more exact.

FORMULAE FOR CALCULATION OF AREA OF PLAIN GEOMETRICAL FIGURES

Right-angled triangle $\dfrac{a \times b}{2}$

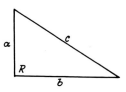

Isosceles triangle $\dfrac{c \times v}{2}$

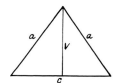

Equilateral triangle $\dfrac{a \times v}{2}$

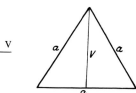

Scalene triangle $\sqrt{(S - a) \times (S - b) \times (S - c)}$

where S = half perimeter =

$$= \dfrac{a + b + c}{2}$$

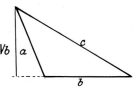

Rectangle $a \times b$

Square	$a \times a = a^2$	*Circle*	$\pi \times r^2$

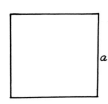
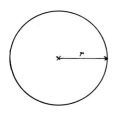

Parallelogram	$a \times v$	*Sector of a circle*	$\dfrac{\pi \times r^2 \times a}{360} = 0.0087 \times r^2 \times a$

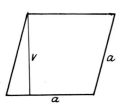

Rhombus	$a \times v$	*Segment of a circle*	$\dfrac{v}{6 \times t} \times (3v^2 + 4t^2)$

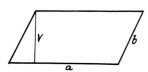

Trapezoid	$\dfrac{a - b}{2} \times v$	*Annulus*	$\pi(r^2_1 - r^2_2)$

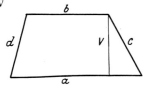
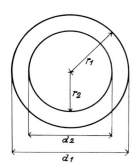

Regular polygon

$\dfrac{1}{2} n \times s \times r$, where

n = number of sides
s = length of side
r = radius of incircle

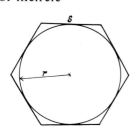

Ellipse	$\dfrac{d \times D \times \pi}{4}$

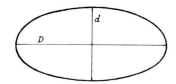

Irregular polygon

$\dfrac{u_1 \times v_1}{2} + \dfrac{u_2 \times v_2}{2} + \dfrac{u_2 \times v_3}{2}$

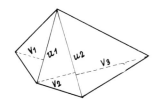

190

FORMULAE FOR CALCULATION OF
VOLUME OF GEOMETRICAL SOLIDS

Cube

$$a \times a \times a = a^3$$

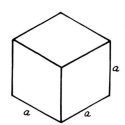

Right parallelepiped

$$a \times b \times c$$

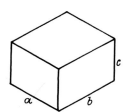

Prism

$$F \times v, \text{ where } F = \text{area of base}$$

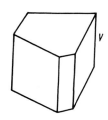

Pyramid

$$\frac{1}{3} F \times v$$

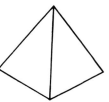

Truncated pyramid

$$\frac{v}{3} \times (F_1 + F_2 + \sqrt{F_1 \times F_2}),$$

where
$F_1 = $ area of bottom base
$F_2 = $ area of top

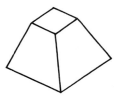

Cone

$$\frac{1}{3} \pi \times r^2 \times v = 1.0472 \times r^2 \times v$$

Truncated cone

$$\frac{\pi \times v}{3} \times (r^2_1 + r^2_2) =$$
$$= 1.0472 \times v \times (r^2_1 + r_1 \times r_2 + r^2_2)$$

Hollow truncated cone

$$\frac{\pi}{2} \times (D_1 + d_1 - 25) \times s \times v,$$

where $s = $ wall thickness

Cylinder

$$\pi \times r^2 \times v$$

Hollow cylinder $\dfrac{\pi \times v}{4} \times (d^2_1 - d^2_2) =$
$$= 0.7854 \times v \times (d^2_1 - d^2_2)$$

For illustration, let us use a few examples. A vase (drawn in full line) is enlarged by ten per cent (drawn in dashed line) in the two diagrams below. The first diagram shows the plotting of a single point on the outline of the enlarged vase; the second shows the whole network of points forming the outline.

The rectangle ABCD enclosing the vase is enlarged along the diagonal to form a rectangle $A_1B_1C_1D_1$. From D-D_1 line **a** is drawn. Its point of intersection with the vase outline (1) is connected with point A by means of line **b**. A parallel line b_1 constructed through point A will intersect line **a** at point 1.

Sphere $\dfrac{4}{3} \times \pi \times r^3 = 4.1888 \times r^3$

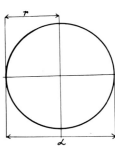

Torus $2 \times \pi^2 \times R \times r^2 = 19.7392 \times R \times r^2$

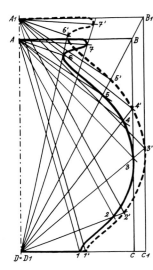

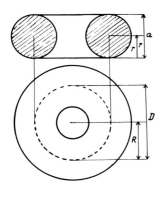

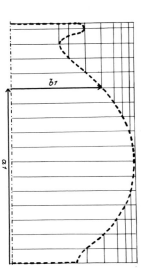

The designs are usually drawn to the same size as the finished article, that is, considering shrinkage due to drying and firing. However, production drawings for pattern makers and manufacturers must be enlarged by the shrinkage of the ceramic batch from which the article is to be made.

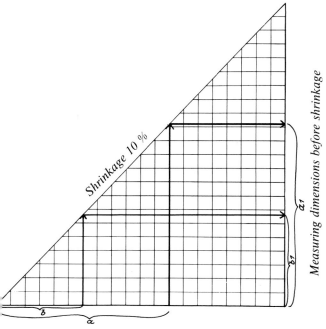

Measuring dimensions after shrinkage

TABLE OF SHRINKAGE COEFFICIENTS

PER CENT SHRINKAGE	COEFFICIENT	PER CENT SHRINKAGE	COEFFICIENT
1.0	1.010	11.0	1.123
1.5	1.015	11.5	1.130
2.0	1.020	12.0	1.136
2.5	1.025	12.5	1.142
3.0	1.031	13.0	1.149
3.5	1.035	13.5	1.155
4.0	1.041	14.0	1.162
4.5	1.047	14.5	1.169
5.0	1.052	15.0	1.176
5.5	1.058	15.5	1.183
6.0	1.064	16.0	1.190
6.5	1.069	16.5	1.198
7.0	1.075	17.0	1.204
7.5	1.081	17.5	1.212
8.0	1.087	18.0	1.219
8.5	1.092	18.5	1.227
9.0	1.098	19.0	1.234
9.5	1.105	19.5	1.242
10.0	1.111	20.0	1.250
10.5	1.117		

The diagram above shows another method of working out the necessary enlargement by using an auxiliary triangle. Naturally, each shrinkage rate requires a different triangle.

The dimensions of the article after shrinkage are ruled out on the triangle base, while the dimensions of the model enlarged by the shrinkage rate are plotted on the perpendicular.

The necessary enlargement may also be calculated from tables. Let us consider the following example: a fired pot should be 30 cm high and its diameter is to be 15 cm. The shrinkage rate of the batch to be used is 12.5 per cent. The table gives the coefficient for 12.5 per cent as 1.142. $30 \times 1.142 = 34.26$ and $15 \times 1.142 = 17.13$. A raw pot should then be 34.26 cm high and its diameter should be 17.13 cm.

In this manner any point measured on the drawing can be calculated.

GLOSSARY

Ball clay
Plastic clay of a dark colour caused by organic matter, firing light to white. The name is derived from the original method of extraction from the ground by which the clay was cut into balls. Used for formulation of batches to give them plasticity.

Balsam
Binding agent for on-glaze colours and enamels.

Barbotine
French term for deflocculated clay (slip). The word derives from *barboter*, i.e. 'trod in mud'.

Bentonite
Highly plastic clay of volcanic origin containing much montmorillonite. Even a small quantity will improve plasticity of ceramic batches. Named after its deposit at Fort Benton, Wyoming, USA.

Bianco sopra bianco (It.)
Literally 'white on white', a term for decoration in opaque white colour on light bluish or greyish tin glaze used in 16th century Italian maiolica and 18th century Delft and Bristol wares.

Biscuit or **bisque** (both Fr.)
A term for unglazed procelain fired at glaze firing temperature. Often used also for any unglazed and fired body.

Biscuit firing
First firing of body without glaze, usually at lower temperatures.

Blanc de Chine (Fr.)
Highly translucent soft Chinese porcelain from the late Ming period, made in Te-hua, Fukien province; white to ivory unpainted figurines and pots with vegetable motifs; much exported to Europe during the 17th and 18th centuries.

Body
Clay used to make ceramic wares.

Bull's blood
see *Sang de boeuf*

Casting slip
Ceramic batch deflocculated with 0.2-0.4% defloculant and a little quantity of water.

Celadon (Fr.)
A term used for special Chinese green glaze of the *Tung-yao* type for stoneware. Used later also by Korean and Japanese potters. Celadon colour is produced by reduction of ferruginous oxides in the glaze. Depending on the quantity of oxide, firing temperature and method of reduction, its shade ranges from greyish green to blue-green. Name derived from the name of the hero of *L'Astrée*, a 17th-century French romance by Honoré D'Urfé, whose protagonist wore clothes of such colour.

Ceramics
All wares made of clay which has undergone chemical changes due to heat in excess of 600 °C.

Chien-yao (Chin.)
Also known as ***temmoku*** (Jap.); stoneware with a dark brown to black glaze, sometimes with oil spot or hare's fur effects.

Chün-yao (Chin.)
A special type of celadon ware (see) of the Sung period. Typical characteristics include grey to greyish blue glazes with red cuprous spots.

Colophony
Alternative name for rosin — a resin obtained from pine trees using distillation or solvent extraction techniques.

Coperta (It.)
Transparent lead glaze over painted decoration on opaque tin glaze in Italian maiolica wares; highly glossy. Called ***kwaart*** on Dutch faience wares.

Crackle glaze
From Fr. *craquelé*, a glaze cracked on purpose for decorative effect.

Crackles
Intentional cracks in glaze, sometimes made more pronounced by colour or china ink.

Crazing
Unintentional cracking of glaze caused by different shrinkage of glaze and body during cooling. See also **Crackles.**

Crystalline glaze
Glaze which on cooling produces crystals resembling patterns produced by frost on windows.

Deflocculant
Liquefying agent such as soda or water glass.

Delft ware
Faience ware with blue Chinoiserie decoration manufactured in Delft, Holland, during the 17th century.

Faenza
Italian city, since the 14th century a major centre of ceramic production. The term **faience** derives from the name which began to be used in France during the 17th century for wares with lead-tin glaze.

Faience
Term used in literature for two different types of ware. Coined in 17th century France to designate porous ware with lead-tin glaze. Later applied also to a completely different type of ware, that is, ancient porous wares of the Middle East, especially Egypt.

Famille (Fr.)
Albert Jacquement, a French art historian of the 19th century, used the word to classify Chinese porcelains according to the combination of base and decoration colours:
Famille jaune (yellow family) = yellow base + decoration
Famille noire (black family) = black-green base + green enamel decoration
Famille rose (pink family) = rose decoration and pink-red enamel decoration
Famille verte (green family) = wares with on-glaze decoration, predominantly transparent green enamels.
The terms are used mainly for porcelain of the K'ang-hsi period (18th century).

Flambé
see **Sang be boeuf**

Flux
Agent facilitating melting and sintering.

Frit
Glassy melt, used as a basic constituent of fritted glazes.

Glaze
Glassy surface coating of ceramic wares.

Glost-firing
The firing of the glaze on to the pre-fired body.

Grog
Admixture lowering plasticity of ceramic clays.

Habaner faience
Seventeenth century wares made in Moravia and Slovakia by Swiss and German Anabaptist immigrants who had settled in the region during the 16th century.

Hare's fur
see **Chien-yao**

High fire colours (Fr. **grand feu**)
Used for colours (overglaze and maiolica colours, porcelain decorations, etc.) fired simultaneously with the glaze at about 1000 °C and higher.

Jiggerer
Operator of a jigger and jolley machine, producing flatware and hollow-ware (see **Jiggering and Jolleying**).

Jiggering and Jolleying
Shaping flatware (jiggering) and hollow-ware (jolleying) on a mechanical device known as **jigger and joley** (see **Jiggerer**).

Kaolin
China clay; term comes from Chinese **kao-ling**, that is, high hill; basic raw material for manufacture of ceramics.

Kiln atmosphere
see **Oxidizing fire, Reduction firing**

Koryo (Kor.)
Korean dynasty (936-1392) concurrent with the Sung and Yüan dynasties of China; characterized by special celadons whose manufacture culminated especially in the early 12th century. Koryo celadons are semi-transparent, darker than Chinese **Kuan** or **Lung-ch'üan** wares.

Kuan-yao (Chin.)
'Imperial ware' manufactured for the Imperial palace during the Sung dynasty.

Local reduction
Method of reducing glazes in oxidizing firing by adding silicon carbide; used especially for copper red.

Long clay
Also known as fat clay, that is, one that is plastic and suitable for modelling.

Low fire colours (Fr. *petit feu*)
Used for colours (on glazes and enamels, etc.) applied on a fired glaze and glost-fired at about 800 °C.

Lung-ch'üan (Chin.)
Centre of ceramic manufacture in the Che-kang province. Term used for typical blue-green celadons of local origins.

Lustre
Metallic iridescent surface of glazes, colours and salt solutions.

Mezzomaiolica (It.)
Semi-maiolica, semi-faience, that is, porous slip-ware, with painted or sgraffito decoration under a transparent lead glaze.

Muffle
Arch built from fireclay bricks inside the kiln to protect wares against direct contact with flame and gases.

Melting point
Temperature at which the raw glaze turns into glass.

Oil spot
Special glaze effect, see *Chien-yao*.

Onion pattern
Cobalt underglaze decoration after Chinese motifs used in Meissen since the 18th century. Formed by lotus blossoms and pomegranates resembling onions in shape.

Open fire kiln
One in which the flames come in contact with wares, for example, bonfire, clamp, ground-hog, brazier and other kiln types.

Oxidizing fire
Implies perfect combustion with surplus of oxygen which causes metals contained in clay and glaze to retain the colour of their oxides.

Pâte-sur-pâte (Fr.)
Literally 'paste on paste', a term for porcelain decoration technique in which a relief design is created on unfired, unglazed body by applying successive layers of white slip with a brush (introduced in 18th-century China, employed at Sèvres c. 1850).

Petuntse, Petunze (Chin.)
Feldspathic rock, a constituent of Chinese porcelains.

Piccolpasso, Cipriano (1524-79)
Italian potter who summarized his knowledge of maiolica manufacture in his treatise *Li tre libri dell'arte del vasajo* (1556-7).

Pink
Carnation red, ceramic colour made from a mixture of chromic, tin and calcium oxides.

Porcelain
Ceramic ware with nonporous body, translucent if thin-walled. Originated in China at the turn of the 9th and 10th centuries. Name is said to have been coined by Marco Polo after an Italian term for shell (*porcella*) which it resembled in appearance.

Proto-porcelain
Ceramic wares from the times of the Han dynasty (2nd century BC), with nontransparent body containing kaolin and feldspar.

Red clay
Ferruginous clay firing red.

Reduction firing
Firing ceramics with reduced access of air, carbon utilizing oxygen from oxides, reduces the latter to lower oxides or pure metals.

Robbia, della
Family of Florentine sculptors of the 15th and 16th centuries. Robbia Luca di Simono di Marco (1399-1482) was the first to have used lead-tin glazes for his sculptures and reliefs.

Run glaze
Very soft glaze which penetrates a regular basic glaze when fired, producing random patterns.

Salt glaze
Special glaze used for stoneware. Forms when rock salt is thrown in fire during the final stage of firing. The sodium oxide thus produced combines with silicon on the surface to produce a thin glaze.

Sang de boeuf (Fr.)
Literally bull's blood, also termed China red or *flambé*; Chinese porcelain and stoneware glazes and their occidental imitations in which copper is reduced to red colour. Other shades of copper red include peach bloom.

Sgraffito
In ceramic usage, a term for decoration scratched in colour or slip to expose body of a different colour.

Short clay
Also known as lean clay, that is in one with low workability, a clay that breaks when modelled.

Slip
Thin ceramic paste.

Slip glaze
Glaze whose only or predominant constituent is a low-melting clay which vitrifies in fire.

Smaltino (It.)
Lavender blue in glaze used in the 15th century by the della Robbia shop, later also elsewhere.

Solitaire (Fr.)
Breakfast service for a single person.

String
Twisted wire used to cut body from the wheel.

Temmoku (Jap.)
see **Chien-yao**

Tête-à-tête service (Fr.)
Breakfast service for two.

Three colour glaze
Also known as 'egg and spinach', a soft lead glaze of various colours applied on each other. Used originally for Chinese burial pottery of the T'ang period.

Thrower
Potter working on a wheel.

Throwing
Shaping of pots on a potter's wheel without the aid of moulds or templates.

Ting-yao (Chin.)
White porcelain from the Sung period (10th to 13th centuries), named after the town in Hopei province. Brown and black glazed *Ting-yao* wares also exist, but are rare.

Trimming
Finishing of leather-hard pots and their bottoms on a wheel.

Tung-yao (Chin.)
Northern celadon, that is, celadon manufactured during the Sung dynasty (960-1279) in northern China. Characteristic is its grey or yellowish stoneware body with engraved relief decoration under an olive green glaze.

Vitrification
Physical and chemical process, whereby high temperature causes small particles to fuse into larger ones, accompanied by partial or total loss of porosity.

Water slip
Clay made liquid with water (60-80%), with no deflocculant.

Yao (Chin.)
Chinese term signifying ceramics, ceramic shops and kilns (see **Tung-yao**, **Ting-yao**, etc.).

Fig. 170   Decorating a leather-hard body with relief produced by wooden mallets (beaters) of various profiles (Professor O. Eckert)

BIBLIOGRAPHY

Artigas, José Llorens: *Formulario y prácticas de cerámica,* Barcelona, 1961

Bárta, Rudolf: *Sklářství a keramika* (Glassmaking and Ceramics), Prague, 1952

Behrens, Richard: *Glaze Projects,* Columbus, 1973

Berdel, Eduard: *Einfaches chemisches Praktikum,* Coburg, 1932

Cardew, Michael: *Pioneer Pottery,* New York, 1969

Chládek, Jiří, et al.: *Dekorace užitkového porcelánu* (Decoration of Utility Porcelain), Prague, 1984

Crespi, David E.: *Ceramic Glaze Formulae,* New Haven, 1967

Dodd, A. E.: *Dictionary of Ceramics,* New Jersey, 1967

Gebauer, Walter: *Kunsthandwerkliche Keramik,* Leipzig, 1980

Grebanier, Joseph.: *Chinese Stoneware Glazes,* New York, 1975

Hegemann, Hans: *Die Herstellung des Porzellans,* Berlin, 1938

Henschkel—Muche: *ABC Keramik,* Leipzig, 1974

Kanhäuser, František: *Teorie a praxe keramické výroby v Československu* (Theory and Practice of Ceramic Manufacture in Czechoslovakia), Prague, 1951

Kenny, J. B.: *The Complete Book of Pottery Making,* New York, 1944

Landsfeld, Heřman: *Lidové hrnčířství a džbánkařství* (Folk Pottery and Jug Making), Prague, 1950

Leach, Bernard: *A Potter's Book,* London, 1954

Lynggaard, Finn: *Pottery Raku Technique,* New York, 1970

Nelson, Glenn C.: *Ceramics,* New York, 1978

Noble, J. V.: *The Techniques of Painted Attic Pottery,* New York, 1965

Passeri, Giambattista: *Histoire des peintures sur majolique,* Paris, 1853

Piccolpasso, Cipriano: *Li tre libri dell'arte del vasajo,* Pesaro, 1879 (3rd ed.)

Pukall, W.: *Grundzüge der Keramik,* Coburg, 1922

Rada, Pravoslav: *Jak se dělá keramika* (Ceramic Making) Prague, 1963

Rada, Pravoslav: *Kniha o technikách keramiky* (The Book of Ceramic Techniques), Prague, 1956

Rathgen, Friedrich: *Die Konservierung von Altertumsfunden,* Berlin, 1926

Sanders, Herbert H.: *The World of Japanese Ceramics,* Tokyo, 1968

Scheufler, Vladimír: *Lidové hrnčířství v českých zemích* (Folk Pottery in Bohemia and Moravia), Prague, 1972

Sprechsaal Kalender 1938, Coburg, 1937

Steinbrecht, Gustav: *Steingut-Fabrikation,* Vienna, 1927

Weiss, Gustav: *Ullstein Fayencenbuch,* Frankfurt, 1970

Weiss, Gustav: *Ullstein Porzellanbuch,* Berlin, 1964

Periodicals

Ceramic Review, London, GB
Ceramic Monthly, Columbus, USA
Keramik Magazin, W. Berlin

LIST OF ILLUSTRATIONS

BLACK-AND-WHITE PLATES

17 *Artichoke and Asparagus* butter dishes. Holíč, Slovakia, 1760—70. Faience with painting on fired glaze; Artichoke turquoise green, Asparagus pale yellow, with green tips, drawing in manganese. Height: Artichoke 15 cm, Asparagus 21 cm. Museum of Decorative Arts, Prague.

18 Pot. Moravia, Czechoslovakia, 1616. Habaner faience with pewter lip and spout, white tin glaze, drawing in cobalt and manganese. Height 26.5 cm. Museum of Decorative Arts, Prague.

19 Cup with sugar bowl. Staffordshire, England, 18th century. Wedgwood ware (black basalt), black coloured body. Height: bowl 14 cm, cup 6.5 cm. Museum of Decorative Arts, Prague.

20 Goblet with lid. Staffordshire, England, 18th century. Wedgwood ware (jasper ware), blue body with white cameo decoration. Height 25 cm. Museum of Decorative Arts, Prague.

21 Pitcher. Bolesław, Poland, 18th century. Stoneware with typical coffee-coloured (Bolesław brown) slip glaze and white reliefs. Height 17.5 cm. Museum of Decorative Arts, Prague.

22 Octagonal box. Ri, Korea, 18th century. Glazed stoneware, white and brown slip. Height 13 cm, diameter 12 cm. National Gallery, Prague.

23 Teapot. Kuan-Tung (Canton), China, 18th century. Unglazed stoneware, dark red body. Length 22 cm. Private collection.

24 *Aleteo.* Gerda Gruber, Mexico, 1980. Bone china, clay with fireclay, wood; electrically fired at 1280 °C. Height 45 cm. Museum of Modern Art, Mexico City.

25 *Psyche.* Royal Porcelain Factory, Copenhagen, Denmark, after 1867. Biscuit porcelain (after a sculpture by B. Thorvaldsen, 1811). Height 31 cm. Museum of Decorative Arts, Prague.

26 Porcelain cube. Imre Schrammel, Hungary, 1982. Biscuit porcelain deformed by a shot from a small calibre pistol while still plastic; gas-fired at 1380 °C. Height 15 cm. Private collection.

27 Chalice with base. Kurt Spurey, Austria, 1983. Porcelain, white base with transparent glaze, brown *temmoku* chalice; electrically fired at 1320 °C. Height 21 cm, diameter 21 cm. Private collection.

28 *Landscape.* Johny Rolf, Netherlands, 1982. Stoneware, ochre body, decorated with white, black, green and ferruginous slip; engraved lines rubbed with black-brown oxides; electrically fired at 1260 °C. Height 32 cm. Private collection.

29 *Column.* Václav Šerák, Czechoslovakia, 1982. Black oxide of manganese body, white semi-matt opalescent glaze; electrically fired at 1100 °C. Height 40 cm. Exhibition of Ceramics, Bechyně, Czechoslovakia.

30 *The Earth.* Peteris Martinsons, Lithuania, USSR, 1980. Stoneware body with fireclay, thin yellow glaze, drawing in black slip and red reduction glaze; wood fired, biscuit at 1200 °C, glaze at 1090 °C under reducing conditions. Diameter 40 cm. Private collection.

31 *Cyclade.* Edouard Chappalaz, Switzerland, 1984. Stoneware, white matt glaze with precipitations; electrically fired at 1280 °C in a reducing atmosphere. 55 × 53 × 22 cm. Private collection.

32 Oval dish. Jean-Claude de Crousaz, Switzerland, 1985. Stoneware with feldspathic glaze, painting on raw glaze; gas-fired at 1300 °C in a reducing atmosphere. 40 × 25 cm. Private collection.

33 Vase in the form of a gold dust bag. A Kyoto master, Japan, 2nd half of 17th century. Stoneware with slip glaze. Height 13.5 cm. National Gallery, Prague.

34 *Owl.* Lubor Těhník, Czechoslovakia, 1983. Black oxide of manganese body, matt white glaze, gold; electrically fired at 1100 °C. Height 32 cm. Private collection.

35 *Green Helmeted Head.* Carmen Dionyse, Belgium, 1984. Whiteware; upper part glazed with matt opalescent white glaze, lower part with turquoise crystalline glaze; electrically fired, biscuit at 1075 °C, glost-fired at 1050 °C. Height 24 cm. Private collection.

36 Pots. Rearen (1584) and Siegburg (3rd quarter of 16th century), Germany. Salt-glazed stoneware, brown and pale grey, with rich relief decoration. Height 34.5 cm. Private collection.

37 Meiping vase. Seto, Japan, 20th century. Stoneware with engraved decoration under olive green. 14th-century *Ko-Seto* glaze. Height 48 cm. National Gallery, Prague.

38 Kuan box. China, Yüan dynasty, 13th-14th century. Stoneware, *Lung Ch'üan-yao* celadon glaze. Height 22 cm.
National Gallery, Prague.

39 Tulip vase. Adrien Kocks, 'De Grieksche A' workshop, Delft, Holland, 1687-1701. Faience with blue decoration. Height 29 cm. Museum of Decorative Arts, Prague.

40 Plate. Casa Pirota, Faenza, Italy, 1540. Maiolica, pale blue glaze painted with *bianco sopra azzuro;* orange figure. Diameter 24.5 cm. Museum of Decorative Arts, Prague.

41 *In a Gallery.* Jindra Viková, Czechoslovakia, 1985. Electroporcelain with relief lugs, combined underglaze and on-glaze painting; electrically fired at 1300 °C. Height 80 cm. Private collection.

42 *Bird,* ritual pipe. Peru, Chimizo culture, 1200-1450. Smoked, partially slicked buff body. 22 × 23 cm. Private collection.

43 *Wet Julia.* Bohuslav Zemánek, Czechoslovakia, 1974. Porous ware clay with fireclay, glazed with white opaque glaze; modelled sculpture was used to make an auxiliary plaster mould which was then hand-pressed with clay; electrically fired at 1100 °C. 80 × 60 cm. Private collection.

44 *Shishi Lion.* Kyoto, Japan, 19th century. Brown stoneware decorated with fine engraving (fur), partially glazed. 20 × 23 cm. Private collection.

45 Candle box. Prachatice district, south Bohemia, first half of 19th century. Unglazed pottery; luted openwork strips used to reinforce walls serve as decoration. 38 × 11.5 × 48 cm. Municipal Museum, Prachatice, Czechoslo-

46 vakia. (Research data by courtesy of Vladimír Scheufler.)

46 Tankard. Altenburg, Germany, 1713. Stoneware with brown glaze, decorated with white stamped relief and quartz pebble pattern, pewter trimming. Height 28 cm. Museum of Decorative Arts, Prague.

47 Headrest. China, 12th century. *Tz'chou yao* stoneware, brownish body with white slip and engraved decoration. 14 × 28 × 16 cm. National Gallery, Prague.

48 Dish. Perugia, Italy, 1500-1520. Mezzomaiolica with decoration engraved in white slip and painted blue, yellow and violet. Diameter 38 cm. Museum of Decorative Arts, Prague.

49 Teapot. Japan, 17th-18th century. Brown stoneware, double body decorated with openwork and rich relief ornamentation. Height 11 cm. Museum of Decorative Arts, Prague.

50 *Odalisque.* Slavkov (Schlaggenwald). Bohemia, 3rd quarter of 19th century. Porcelain lithophane (negative and positive views). Length 18.5 cm. Museum of Decorative Arts, Prague.

51 Plate. Bohemia, 18th century. Faience with blue trailed slip. Diameter 33 cm. Ethnographical Museum, Prague.

52 Dish. Modra, Slovakia, early 20th century. Pottery, white slip with blue and light brown trailed slip, transparent glaze. Diameter 27.5 cm. Ethnographical Museum, Prague.

53 Dish. South Bohemia, early 18th century. Pottery, blue glaze with white marbling. Diameter 28 cm. Ethnographical Museum, Prague.

54 Dish. South Bohemia, early 18th century. Pottery, blue glaze with white trailed slip. Diameter 28 cm. Ethnographical Museum, Prague.

55 Milk cooler. Kralovice, Bohemia, 1870-90. Pottery, brown glaze, white marbling. Height 19 cm. Municipal Museum, Kralovice, Czechoslovakia. (Research data by courtesy of Vladimír Scheufler.)

56 *Wave Variation — Ripple,* dish. Eileen Lewenstein, England, 1983. White stoneware with dark blue and pale green slip and drawing in black pastel; electrically fired at 1245 °C. Private collection.

57 Plate. Jindřichův Hradec district, Bohemia, 1693. Mezzomaiolica, buff body, blue slip, engraved decoration, transparent glaze. Diameter 28 cm. Ethnographical Museum, Prague.

58 Dish. Creil, France, 1810. Stoneware with Ranston landscape printed in black. 24 × 24 cm. Museum of Decorative Arts, Prague.

59 *Gentleman with Rose in Lapel.* Pravoslav Rada, Czechoslovakia, 1983. Porcelain, photographic collage, silk screen printed on fired glaze; black, flower red and green; oil fired at 1340 °C, decoration at 800 °C. Diameter 30 cm. Private collection.

60 Kiln model. China, Han dynasty, 1st century AD. Pottery with iridescent lead glaze. 14 × 18 × 25 cm. National Gallery, Prague.

61 Ikebana vase in the form of a fireman's bucket. Sakata Tomiya, 13th master of the Hagi workshop, Japan, 20th century. Stoneware, celadon glaze. Height 30.5 cm. National Gallery, Prague.

62 Tile with St George. Bohemia, 15th century. Unglazed pottery, hand-pressed in a wooden mould. 18 × 18 cm. Museum of Decorative Arts, Prague.

Index

Numbers in *italics* refer to illustration captions

205